MW01515049

"YOU CAN THE MAGIC IN YOUR LIFE. HOW DO I KNOW? I'M LIVING PROOF!"

Bob Garner knows what it takes to turn dreams into reality. Years ago, he dreamed about creating a company that would combine his interest in business with his love for the arts of magic and mindreading . . . and his innate desire to make people laugh. Out of high school and with little money, Garner passionately began to study the lives and strategies of successful people. Applying the principles that he discovered, he developed his own formula for excellence—and soon his dream took flight.

Today, Garner's dream is a reality. As President of Motivative & Communicative Concepts, his client list features numerous Fortune 500 corporations and leading associations, and he has logged an impressive twenty years of experience as a successful entrepreneur and businessperson. His company specializes in producing live presentations that blend specific business issues, concerns, and goals with astonishing demonstrations of magic, mindreading, comedy, and audience participation at meetings, conferences, trade shows, and events worldwide. He and his team of presentation specialists use these entertaining demonstrations as highly creative audio/visual tools—producing a learning environment that is informative, inspirational, exciting, and fun. Their unique presentations have stimulated the sales of millions of dollars in clients' goods and services.

Additionally, the media recognizes Garner as an expert on sales, communication, presentation techniques, and motivation. His articles have appeared in many trade journals and magazines for a variety of industries, and he is a welcome guest on numerous radio and television talk shows.

Having achieved financial and personal success, Garner's mission is focused on helping others do the same. A dynamic speaker, his *Make the Magic Happen*™ program and other inspirational materials are helping countless people create more powerful and productive lives.

Garner is a member of the Association for Training and Development (ASTD), the Publisher's Marketing Association (PMA), the International Brotherhood of Magicians (IBM), and the American Society for Psychical Research (ASPR).

Garner and his wife/business partner, Marleta, live on the beautiful Central Coast of California in San Luis Obispo.

For information on Bob Garner's motivational program, *Make the Magic Happen*™, or other educational and inspirational material, visit *www.bobgarner.com* or call 805-534-1576.

"A roadmap for success and life."
—Jeannine D. Richison, PH.D., California Polytechnic
State University, San Luis Obispo, CA

Regardless of your profession, age, depth of education,
financial situation, or socio-economic environment,
Masters of Motivation has a message for you.
Take a journey that will change your life.

"Dive into this treasure chest of insights and inspiration."
—Freddie Ravel, #1 International Recording Star
and creator of *Tune Up to Success*™

Masters of Motivation is crammed encyclopedically with
knowledge of ways to move successfully toward dreamed
about goals in life. Persons locked in by shyness, timidity,
fear, or super-caution may well find just the right keys
here to free them from their psychological or physical
prison." —The Rev. Dr. John Nicholls Booth

"There is an old saying, 'God may have a plan but unless
we do something about it, nothing is going to happen!'
Masters of Motivation motivates your mind to do something with your thoughts, your life, your attitude, and your
purpose in living."
—Rev. Canon Wm. V. Rauscher, Episcopal clergyman,
honorary Canon of Trinity Cathedral,
Trenton, NJ, author, and lecturer

"I highly recommend *Masters of Motivation* to anyone in
sales. Thank you for making these treasures available to
the next generation of super achievers."
—Holly Forsyth, pharmaceutical sales representative

"As a woman and entrepreneur, I found the advice and ideas in *Masters of Motivation* to be not only useful, but also empowering and encouraging."
—**Susan K. Polk, President, Polk Insurance**

"I can pick up this book, turn to any section, and within a few minutes, I can feel myself becoming more confident and inspired. I look at the present and toward the future with faith, patience and renewed power."
—**Brian Mackowiak, entrepreneur,**
BMAC Web Designs

"I have spent thousands of hours working with at-risk and troubled young adults. Not only will *Masters of Motivation* provide a blueprint to help them become responsible and successful young adults, but it also provides me with inspiration and guidance."
—**King Ayettey Zubaidah, mentor of at-risk youth**

"*Masters of Motivation* provides excellent direction for at-risk youth and a valuable resource to their teachers and counselors."
—**Sid Richison, Assistant Superintendent, Personnel,**
Lucia Mar Unified School District

DEDICATION

This book is dedicated to my wife, Marleta Warneke-Garner, whose assistance—as well as kindness, under-standing and unrelenting belief and support—has allowed the magic to happen in my life.

I love you,

—Bob

In memory of C.E. "Bert" Warneke, an educator and counselor whose simple and eloquent words of advice inspired hundreds of young people—as well as his wife Lillian, his daughter Marleta, and myself—
to reach for the stars.

MASTERS
OF
MOTIVATION

CLASSIC WORDS OF WISDOM
BY THREE MEN WHO INSPIRED
MILLIONS TO SUCCESS

COMPILED & EDITED
BY BOB GARNER

Sunday & Weiss Publishing
Los Osos, CA

Published by:
Sunday & Weiss Publishing
P.O. Box 6001
Los Osos, CA 93412
Orders@sundayandweiss.com

First Edition 2004

ISBN: 0-9744424-5-3
Library of Congress Control Number: 2003096229
Category: Business/Self Help

Assistant editor: Marleta Warneke-Garner
Proofreader: Susan Stewart
Illustrations by: Emily Olson
Cover and Interior Design: Lightbourne, Inc.
Printer: DeHart's Printing Services

Printed in the United States of America

TABLE OF CONTENTS

A MESSAGE FROM BOB GARNER

**You are about to embark on a
journey that will change your life.**

Over the years, millions of men and women have taken that same journey. What they found at the end was inspiration, confidence, and power, as well as a burning desire to "make the magic happen" in their lives and the lives of others.

And make the magic happen, they did. Lives were changed, millionaires were made, businesses were started, associations were founded, careers were saved, and much more. Whatever was the main thrust of their desire—these adventurers achieved it. The stories of success and happiness that have been attributed to that journey would fill a library.

How do I know? I have spent countless years studying the lives of successful people. My business and speaking engagements have allowed me to personally speak with presidents of the United States, Fortune 100, 500, and association executives, leading sports personalities and celebrities, as well as top sales people, employees and entrepreneurs in 48 states and 16 countries. Among the many common denominators of these super-achievers, there is one that stands out—the majority ascribe a great part of their success to the universal teachings that you will find in *Masters of Motivation*.

Additionally, I am also living proof that the journey that lies ahead for you can turn your dreams into reality, and I attribute much of my success, wealth, and happiness to the principles and teachings found in this book.

Now YOU have the same opportunity to take that journey. I urge you to take it. It will change your life.

Though the focus of *Masters of Motivation* is directed at men and women who would like to become more successful in the business world—much of the information can be used by anyone.

Dear reader, this book is about helping you achieve your dreams. And it doesn't matter what the economy or your current financial situation may be or your health, age, depth of education, or socio-economic environment. All that matters is that you really "WANT TO" take this journey and that you "WANT TO" listen and apply the wisdom and principles that your guides have calmly waited over a hundred years to tell you.

United for the first time in one volume, your guides are three of the earliest inspirational writers and speakers upon which many motivational writers and speakers have relied to produce their own work.

Your first guide is James Allen. By some, he is considered a "mystic"; by others, a philosopher. Regardless of the moniker, Allen wrote what is considered the very first motivational book *As a Man Thinketh*. In essence, it is a treatise based on the principle of the power of your thoughts and how those thoughts relate to your overall life. He clearly explains how you are in control of what you think, and how by choosing the right thoughts, you can create the life that you desire—or by choosing the wrong thoughts, create a life that you despair.

I chose Allen to be your first guide, because through numerous readings of *As a Man Thinketh*, I came to understand: Your thoughts shape the circumstances that direct your destiny. Until you come to a similar understanding, you will not be able to apply the teachings in this book or most likely any other inspirational piece of work. Nor will you learn how powerful your thoughts are and how they can help you attain anything you *truly* desire.

James Allen will show you how to develop and use the power of your thoughts. Immediately you will notice results. Life changing opportunities will appear, as if by magic, and you will possess the knowledge, power, and confidence to grab them. As you begin to create your new life, others will be amazed at your progress and success. Your friends and associates will stand in awe as they witness you taking what you want out of life, instead of taking what life gives you. I guarantee you that once you read and apply Allen's teachings, your life will never be the same again.

Your second guide is P.T. Barnum—one of the most astute businesspersons, entrepreneurs, and showmen who ever lived. And before I continue, I must state that Barnum never said, "There is a sucker born every minute," or anything even close to that erroneously credited phrase. It was actually said by a competitor who was jealous of Barnum's success.

P.T. Barnum wrote what many consider to be the bible of business success, *The Art of Money-Getting* (which today would be titled, "The Art of Asset Procurement"). In *The Art of Money-Getting*, Barnum shows you the power of economizing and the value of saving money. Additionally, he offers his ideas and principles on how to start, run, and maintain a successful business.

However, if you don't want to have your own business, *The Art of Money-Getting* still contains a treasure chest of information. Barnum shares with you the secrets on how to: gain employment and stay employed; be a better employer; retain key employees, and become a more effective leader, as well as snippets on customer service, perseverance, advertising, integrity, and much more.

The reason I chose Barnum to be your second guide is that in *The Art of Money-Getting*, Barnum provides you with accurate information on how to achieve success in the world of business. Anyone, regardless of their profession—salespeople, doctors, lawyers, executives, small business owners, managers, front-line employees, butchers, bakers or candlestick makers—can learn how to become more productive and increase their wealth from reading and applying the principles that are found in *The Art of Money-Getting*. And let me tell you, in *The Art of Money-Getting*, you will not be reading "theories and techniques," but real world experiences that has made millionaires out of many followers of the teachings of P.T. Barnum.

Your third and final guide is Russell Conwell. Conwell was a brilliant orator, businessperson, minister, and philanthropist. He created his speech *Acres of Diamonds* primarily to address the varied excuses people had for not succeeding back in the 1800s. Strangely, these are the same excuses people use today in the 21st century. With his own unique style of delivery, Conwell squashed each excuse with logical, applicable examples. He also took "aim" at people who constantly "put down" their town or city in which they lived. Replace the word "Philadelphia" with any town, city, state, or country and you will discover how right on "target" Conwell was . . . and still is. Conwell helped people understand that they didn't have to search elsewhere to find the riches they desired. Instead, he told his listeners that their riches could be found in their own backyards and within themselves.

Conwell emphatically told his audiences that becoming

wealthy was good. Yet, he was also equally assertive in telling them that after they had become wealthy, they had a duty to give back to the people and the community in which they had achieved their wealth and—if it were not the same—the community in which they lived.

The reason I chose Conwell for your last guide is two-fold. First, he attacks the negative thoughts that you might think about business and making money. Secondly, and more importantly, his ideas on acquiring success also include the necessity of "giving back."

There is a message for everyone in *Acres of Diamonds*.

United for the first time in one easy to read volume, *Masters of Motivation* systematically lets Allen, Barnum, and Conwell guide you on your new journey. In *As a Man Thinketh*, you will learn how to use the power of your thoughts to achieve anything of which you can dream. In *The Art of Money-Getting*, you will learn how to capitalize on those thoughts to acquire business success. In *Acres of Diamonds*, you will learn that many of the "myths" with regard to becoming successful and wealthy are just that . . . "myths." And you will learn that as you become more successful—as you will from applying the principles in this book—that you must give back to those who share your community and your world.

Additionally, you can turn to any page in *Masters of Motivation* and within a few minutes, read a quotation, a thought, or a statement that will empower and ignite your passion to achieve whatever it is you truly desire.

You really are about to embark on a journey that will change your life. I hope that you take it. Because I know that if you do, you will . . . Make the Magic Happen!

—**Bob Garner**

ABOUT THE REVISION

James Allen, P.T. Barnum, and Russell Conwell were born in the late 19th century and—with the exception of Barnum—died in the early 20th century. These men wrote the essays and speeches contained in this volume long before the women's suffrage movement would emancipate women and long before it was politically incorrect to use male pronouns for both genders. Therefore, we have done our best in this revision to include the feminine gender, wherever possible, in all three.

In James Allen's, *As a Man Thinketh*, we made a slight exception. This work was heavily swayed toward the male gender, so to "even it out a bit," we used the male pronoun to include both genders in Chapters 1, 5 and 7; and the female pronoun to include both genders in Chapters 2 and 4. Chapters 3 and 6 have been modified to include both genders. We have left the male pronoun in the title in deference to the author.

In *Acres of Diamonds*, Conwell—who, as mentioned earlier, was a great minister—included a number of references to his spiritual beliefs (Christianity) throughout his speech. In his day—and to a lesser or greater extent today, depending on your view—the Christian inclusions were accepted by some and tolerated or despised by others. If you so choose, the Christian terminology in Conwell's speech can be replaced with those of Judaism, Islam, Buddhism, or any other religious or spiritual wording. If that were done, I feel the message would still be the same. However, to remove all of Conwell's original Christian references from this work would, I believe, diminish some of the thunder, as well as the tone and flow of Conwell's oratorical skills. Therefore, the majority of *Acres of Diamonds* has been left as Conwell would have said it and his listeners would have heard it many years ago. There is still a message for everyone in *Acres of Diamonds*.

Additionally, the rules of grammar and punctuation were slightly different over a hundred years ago than they are today; however, only when it was necessary for ease of reading did we change any words or punctuation from the original text.

JAMES ALLEN
A BIOGRAPHY

James Allen is to many people a mystic, a spiritual guide, and some might even say, a prophet. His works have inspired countless numbers of people, yet so little is known of the man himself.

What is known is that Allen was born in Leicester, England on November 28, 1864. His family was poor, and by the time Allen reached his mid-teens, the family business had run into financial trouble. Allen's father decided that he could better provide for his family by going to America to find work. The plan was for Allen's father to go to America and, once established, send for his family to join him. This plan had worked for countless Europeans, but unfortunately, it didn't work for the Allen family. Shortly after arriving in America, Allen's father was murdered.

James, now only 15 years old, became the family breadwinner. He quit school and took a job as an administrative assistant at a large company in England. It was during this time that James Allen came under the spell of Count Leo Tolstoy, the famous Russian novelist. Tolstoy's pursuit of a simple life, spirituality, and self-discipline appealed to Allen deeply. Over the years, Allen's life began to change from that of the busy employee—trying to earn an income and advance up the company ranks—to the contemplative and meditative life of a writer.

At the age of 38, Allen quit his job and, along with his new wife, moved to Ilfracombe on England's southwest coast. Ilfracombe was a quiet and serene seaside village where the waves of the ocean and rolling grassy hills meet—a location especially conducive for writing.

During the next 10 years, Allen wrote 19 books; however, the one that he is most known for is his second book and masterpiece, *As A Man Thinketh*. *As A Man Thinketh* is based on the concept that through the power of his or her thoughts, a person can achieve all the good and positive things that life has to offer, as well as all the bad and negative things. In short, it is what and how a person thinks that determines a life of wealth, health, and happiness, or poverty, disease, and despair. The foundation of this principle is the Law of Cause and Effect, which asserts that for every "effect" or "happening" there was first a "cause" or "reason" that created the effect. Allen believed that every cause was first—to use Allen's analogy—"planted" and "harvested" in the mind. In other words, the cause or reason initially began as a thought.

Allen never suggested that his concept was an original idea. In fact, in the forward to *As A Man Thinketh*, Allen states, "This little volume (the result of meditation and experience) is not intended as an exhaustive treatise on the much written upon subject of the power of thought." Allen was surely acquainted with the teachings in the Bible, where, for example, in the book of Proverbs, Chapter 23, Verse 7 it is written, "As you think, so shall you be." Allen was also undoubtedly cognizant of the teachings of

Buddha, which state, "All that we are is the result of what we have thought." Yet, it was Allen's precise focus on this one principle, as well as his simple and eloquent explanation of the concept, that has allowed *As A Man Thinketh* to stand the test of time. Allen wrote clearly and concisely, so that all could understand and profit from the "single message."

Those who knew Allen described him as a meditative person—one who lived a simple life, enjoyed walks in the hills, and found peace in gardening and solitude. He would quiet himself, and then write what came to him. Some might state that this "mystical" approach to life allowed for a deeper understanding of the Laws of the Universe and that his writing was almost that of autosuggestion—spiritually guided writing.

Regardless of how he received his information, *As A Man Thinketh* has inspired, motivated, and enhanced the lives of millions. Even today, numerous people claim that this book has opened the door for them to achieve success, health, wealth, and happiness.

For Allen himself, that would not be the case. As it is written in Luke Chapter 4, Verse 24, "No prophet is accepted in his own country." *As A Man Thinketh*, as well as his other writings, never provided Allen with wealth or the notoriety that has been given to him and his works today. He died in 1912 at the age of 48, virtually unknown. Perhaps for Allen, that was what he wanted.

Allen once wrote, "And I dreamed of writing books which would help men and women, whether rich or poor, learned or unlearned, worldly or unworldly to find within themselves the source of all success, all happiness, accomplishment, all truth. And the dream remained with me, and at last became substantial; and now I send forth these books into the world on a mission of healing and blessedness, knowing that they cannot fail to reach the homes and hearts of those who are waiting and ready to receive them."

Hopefully, this edition of *As A Man Thinketh* will allow Allen's dream to move one step closer to reality.

AS A MAN THINKETH

BY JAMES ALLEN

FOREWORD

This little volume (the result of meditation and experience) is not intended as an exhaustive treatise on the much written upon subject of the power of thought. It is suggestive rather than explanatory. Its object being to stimulate men and women to the discovery and perception of the truth that "They themselves are makers of themselves" by virtue of the thoughts which they choose and encourage; that the mind is the master weaver, both of the inner garment of character and the outer garment of circumstance, and that, as they may have woven in ignorance and pain, they may now weave in enlightenment and happiness.

James Allen
Ilfracombe, England

CHAPTER 1

THOUGHT AND CHARACTER

As a man thinketh in his heart, so shall he be, not only embraces the whole of a man's being, but is so comprehensive as to reach out to every condition and circumstance of his life. A man is literally what he thinks; his character being the complete sum of all his thoughts. As the plant springs from and could not be without the seed, so evcry act of a man springs from the hidden seeds of thought, and the act could not have appeared without them.

This applies equally to those acts called "spontaneous" and "unpremeditated" as to those that are deliberately executed.

Act is the blossom of thought, and joy and suffering are its fruit; thus does a man garner in the sweet and bitter fruitage of his own husbandry. Thought in the mind hath made us. If a man's mind hath evil thought, pain comes to him as comes the ox before the wheel. If one endures in purity of thought, joy follows him as his own shadow.

A man is a growth by law, and not a creation by artifice, and cause and effect are as absolute and undeviating in the hidden realm of thought as in the world of visible and material things. A noble and God-like character is not a

thing of favor or chance, but is the natural result of continued effort in right thinking, the effect of a long-cher-
ished association with God-like thoughts. A dishonorable
and depraved character, by the same process, is the result
of the continued harboring of groveling thoughts.

A man is made or unmade by himself. In the armory of
thought he forges the weapons by which he destroys himself. A man also fashions the tools with which he builds for
himself heavenly mansions of joy and strength and peace.
By the right choice and true application of thought, a man
ascends to the divine perfection. By the abuse and wrong
application of thought, a man descends below the level of
the beast. Between these two extremes are all the grades of
character, and a man is their maker and master.

Of all the beautiful truths pertaining to the soul which
have been restored and brought to light in this age, none
is more gladdening or fruitful of divine promise and confidence than this: that a man is the master of thought, the
molder of character, and the maker and shaper of his condition, environment, and destiny.

As a being of power, intelligence, and love, and the lord
of his own thoughts, a man holds the key to every situation, and contains within himself that transforming and
regenerative agency by which he may make himself what
he will. A man is always the master, even in his weakest
and most abandoned state. But in his weakness and
degradation, he is a foolish master who misgoverns his
household.

When he begins to reflect upon his condition and
search diligently for the law upon which his being is
established, he then becomes the wise master, directing
his energies with intelligence and fashioning his thoughts
to fruitful issues. Such is the conscious master, and a man

can only thus become a conscious master by discovering within himself the laws of thought.

This discovery is totally a matter of application, self-analysis, and experience. Only by much searching and mining are gold and diamonds obtained, and a man can find every truth connected with his being, if he will dig deep into the mine of his soul. That he is the maker of his character, the molder of his life, and the builder of his destiny, he may unerringly prove, if he will watch, control, and alter his thoughts, tracing their effects upon himself, upon others and upon his life and circumstances, linking cause and effect by patient practice and investigation. And he will utilize his every experience, even the most trivial, everyday occurrence, as a means of obtaining that knowledge of himself which is understanding, wisdom, and power.

In this direction, as in no other, is the law absolute that "Those that seeketh findeth; and to they that knocketh, it shall be opened." For only by patience, practice, and ceaseless persistence can a man enter the door of the temple of knowledge.

CHAPTER 2

EFFECT OF THOUGHT ON CIRCUMSTANCES

A woman's mind may be likened to a garden, which may be intelligently cultivated or allowed to run wild; but whether cultivated or neglected, it must and will bring forth. If no useful seeds are put into it, then an abundance of useless seeds will fall therein, and will continue to produce their kind.

Just as a gardener cultivates her plot, keeping it free from weeds, and growing the flowers and fruits which she requires, so may a woman tend the garden of her mind, weeding out all the wrong, useless and impure thoughts, and cultivating toward perfection the flowers and fruits of right, useful and pure thoughts.

By pursuing this process, a woman sooner or later discovers that she is the master gardener of her own soul, the director of her own life. It reveals to her the flaws of her thoughts, and helps her to understand, with ever-increasing accuracy, how the thought forces and mind elements operate in the shaping of character, circumstances, and destiny.

Thought and character are one, and as character can only manifest and discover itself through environment and circumstance, the outer conditions of a woman's life will always be found to be harmoniously related to her inner state. This does not mean that a woman's circumstances at any given time are an indication of her entire character, but that those circumstances are so intimately connected with some vital thought element within her that, for the time being, they are indispensable to her development.

Every woman is where she is by the law of her being. The thoughts, which she has built into her character, have brought her there, and in the arrangement of her life, there is no element of chance, but all is the result of a law, which cannot err. This is just as true of those who feel "out of harmony" with their surroundings, as of those who are contented with them.

As a progressive and evolving being, a woman is where she is so that she may learn and grow. And as she learns the spiritual lesson which any circumstance contains for her, it passes away and gives place to other circumstances.

A woman is buffeted by circumstances so long as she believes herself to be the creature of outside conditions. Yet, when she realizes that she is a creative power and that she may command the hidden soil and seeds of her being out of which circumstances grow, she then becomes the rightful master of herself.

That circumstances grow out of thought, every woman knows who has, for any length of time, practiced self-control and self-purification. She would have noticed that the alteration in her circumstances has been in exact ratio with her altered mental condition.

So true is this that when a woman earnestly applies herself to remedy the defects in her character, and makes swift and marked progress, she passes rapidly through a succession of changes. The soul attracts that which it secretly harbors, that which it loves, and also that which it fears. It reaches the height of its cherished aspirations; it falls to the level of its impure desires, and circumstances are the means by which the soul receives its own. Every thought-seed sown or allowed to fall into the mind, and to take root there, produces its own, blossoming sooner or later into act, and bearing its own fruit of opportunity and circumstance. Good thoughts bear good fruit; bad thoughts, bad fruit.

The outer world of circumstances shapes itself to the inner world of thought, and both pleasant and unpleasant external conditions are factors that make for the ultimate good of the individual. As the reaper of her own harvest, a woman learns both of suffering and of bliss. Following the inmost desires, aspirations, and thoughts by which she allows herself to be dominated—whether impure imaginings or thoughts of strong and high endeavor, a woman at last arrives at her fruition and fulfillment in the outer conditions of her life.

A woman does not come to the poor house or the jail by the tyranny of fate or circumstance, but by the pathway of groveling thoughts and base desires. Nor does a pure-minded woman fall suddenly into crime by stress of any mere external force. The criminal thought had long been secretly fostered in the heart, and the hour of opportunity revealed its gathered power.

Circumstances do not make the woman; it reveals her. No such conditions can exist as descending into vice and its accompanying problems and sufferings apart from vicious inclinations. No such conditions can exist as ascending into virtue and its pure happiness without the continued cultivation of virtuous aspirations. A woman, therefore, as the lord and master of thought, is the maker of herself and the shaper of and author of her own environment.

Even at birth, the soul comes of its own and through every step of its earthly pilgrimage it attracts those combinations of conditions which reveal itself, which are the reflections of its own purity and impurity, its strength and weakness. People do not attract that which they want, but that which they are. Their whims, fancies, and ambitions are thwarted at every step, but their inmost thoughts and desires are fed with their own food, be it foul or clean.

People are manacled only by themselves; thought and action are the jailers of Fate. They imprison, being base; they are also the angels of Freedom; they liberate, being noble. Not what she wishes and prays for does a woman get, but what she justly earns. Her wishes and prayers are only gratified and answered when they harmonize with her thoughts and actions.

In the light of this truth, what then, is the meaning of "fighting against circumstances?" It means that a woman is continually revolting against an effect without, while all the time she is nourishing and preserving its cause in her heart. That cause may take the form of a conscious vice or an unconscious weakness; but whatever it is, it stubbornly retards the efforts of its possessor, and thus calls aloud for remedy.

People are anxious to improve their circumstances, but are unwilling to improve themselves; they therefore remain bound. The woman who does not shrink from self-crucifixion can never fail to accomplish the object upon which her heart is set. This is as true of earthly as of heavenly things. Even the woman whose sole object is to acquire wealth must be prepared to make great personal sacrifices before she can accomplish this object; and how much more so is the woman who would realize a strong and well-poised life?

Here is a woman who is wretchedly poor. She is extremely anxious that her surroundings and home comforts should improve, yet all the time she shirks her work, and considers she is justified in trying to deceive her employer on the ground of the insufficiency of her wages. Such a woman does not understand the simplest rudiments of those principles which are the basis of true prosperity, and is not only totally unfit to rise out of her wretchedness, but is actually attracting to herself a still deeper wretchedness by dwelling in, and acting out, shiftless, deceptive, and unkind thoughts.

Here is a rich woman who is the victim of a painful and persistent disease as the result of overeating. This woman is willing to give large sums of money to get rid of her pain, but will not sacrifice her gluttonous desircs. This woman wants to gratify her taste for rich and unnatural foods and have her health as well.

Such a woman is totally unfit to have health, because she has not yet learned the first principles of a healthy life. Here is an employer of labor who adopts crooked measures to avoid paying the minimum wage, and in the hope of making larger profits, reduces the wages of her workers. Such a woman is altogether unfit for prosperity. And when this employer becomes bankrupt, both as regards to reputation and riches, this employer blames circumstances, as opposed to the sole author of the condition—herself.

I have introduced these three cases merely as examples of the truth that each woman is the cause (though nearly always unconsciously) of her own circumstances, and that, while aiming at the good end, she is continually frustrating her accomplishment by encouraging thoughts and desires which cannot possibly harmonize with that end.

Such cases could be multiplied and varied almost indefinitely, but this is not necessary. The reader can, if she so resolves, trace the action of the laws of thought in her own mind and life, and until this is done, mere external facts cannot serve as a ground of reasoning. Circumstances, however, are so complicated, thought is so deeply rooted, and the conditions of happiness vary so vastly with individuals that a woman's entire soul condition (although she may know it) cannot be judged by another from the external aspect of her life alone. A woman may be honest in certain directions, yet suffer privations. A woman may be dishonest in certain directions, yet acquire wealth.

But, the conclusion usually formed that one woman fails because of her particular honesty, and that another woman will prosper because of her particular dishonesty, is the result of a superficial judgment. This judgment is based on the assumption that the dishonest woman is almost totally corrupt, and that the honest woman almost entirely virtuous. In the light of a deeper knowledge and wider experience, such judgment is found erroneous. The dishonest woman may have some admirable virtues which the other does not possess; and the honest woman obnoxious vices, which are absent in the other. The honest woman reaps the good results of her honest thoughts and acts; she also brings upon herself the sufferings that her vices produce. The dishonest woman, likewise, garners her own suffering and happiness.

It is pleasing to human vanity to believe that one suffers because of one's virtue. But not until a woman has pulled up, by the roots, every sickly, bitter, and impure thought from her soul, can that woman be in a position to know and declare that her sufferings are the result of her good, and not of her bad qualities. And on the way to, yet long before she has reached that supreme perfection, she will have found, working in her mind and life, the great law which is absolutely just: You cannot give good for evil and evil for good.

Possessed of such knowledge, she will then know, looking back upon her past ignorance and blindness, that her life is, and always was, justly ordered, and that all her past experiences, good and bad, were the equitable out-working of her evolving, yet un-evolved self.

Good thoughts and actions can never produce bad results; bad thoughts and actions can never produce good results. This is but saying that nothing can come from corn but corn, nothing from apples but apples. People understand this law in the natural world, and work with it; but few understand it in the mental and moral world (though its operation there is just as simple and undeviating), and they, therefore, do not cooperate with it.

Suffering is always the effect of wrong thought in some direction. It is an indication that the individual is out of harmony with herself, with the law of her being. The sole and supreme use of suffering is to purify, to burn out all that is useless and impure. Suffering ceases for a woman who is pure. There could be no object in burning gold after the debris had been removed, and a perfectly pure and enlightened being could not suffer.

The circumstances that a woman encounters with suffering are the result of her own mental disharmony. The circumstances that a woman encounters with blessings are the result of her own mental harmony. Blessings and peace, not material possessions, is the measure of right thought. Wretchedness, not lack of material possessions, is the measure of wrong thought. A woman may be cursed and rich; she may be blessed and poor. Blessings and riches are only joined together when the riches are rightly and wisely used. And the poor woman only descends into wretchedness when she regards her lot as a burden unjustly imposed.

Indigence and indulgence are the two extremes of wretchedness. They are both equally unnatural and the result of mental disorder. A woman is not rightly conditioned until she is a happy, healthy, and prosperous being; and happiness, health, and prosperity are the result of a harmonious adjustment of the inner with the outer of the woman with her surroundings.

A woman only begins to be a woman when she ceases to whine, and commences to search for the hidden justice that regulates her life. And when a woman adapts her mind to that regulating factor, she ceases to accuse others as the cause of her condition. She builds herself up in strong and noble thoughts; she ceases to kick against circumstances, but begins to use these circumstances as aids to her more rapid progress. She uses these circumstances as a means of discovering the hidden powers and possibilities within herself.

Law, not confusion, is the dominating principle in the universe; justice, not injustice, is the soul and substance of life. Righteousness, not corruption, is the molding and moving force in the spiritual government of the world. This being so, a woman has but to right herself to find that the universe is right. And during the process of putting herself right, she will find that as she alters her thoughts towards things and other people, things and other people will alter towards her. The proof of this truth is in every woman, and it therefore admits easy investigation by systematic introspection and self-analysis. Let a woman radically alter her thoughts, and she will be astonished at the rapid transformation it will effect in the material conditions of her life.

People imagine that thought can be kept secret, but it cannot. It rapidly crystallizes into habit, and habit solidifies into circumstance. Bestial thoughts crystallize into habits of drunkenness and sensuality, which solidify into circumstances of destitution and disease. Impure thoughts of every kind crystallize into unbearable and confusing habits, which solidify into distracting and adverse circumstances. Thoughts of fear, doubt, and indecision crystallize into weak, self-deprecating, and indecisive habits, which solidify into circumstances of failure, indigence, and slavish dependence.

Lazy thoughts crystallize into weak habits of uncleanness and dishonesty, which solidify into circumstances of foulness and destitution. Hateful and condemnatory thoughts crystallize into habits of accusation and violence, which solidify into circumstances of injury and persecution. Selfish thoughts of all kinds crystallize into habits of self-seeking, which solidify into distressful circumstances.

On the other hand, beautiful thoughts of all kinds crystallize into habits of grace and kindliness, which solidify into genial and sunny circumstances. Pure thoughts crystallize into habits of temperance and self-control, which solidify into circumstances of repose and peace. Thoughts of courage, self-reliance, and decision crystallize into personable habits, which solidify into circumstances of success, plenty, and freedom. Energetic thoughts crystallize into habits of cleanliness and industry, which solidify into circumstances of pleasantness. Gentle and forgiving thoughts crystallize into habits of gentleness, which solidify into protective and preservative circumstances. Loving and unselfish thoughts solidify into circumstances of sure and abiding prosperity and true riches.

A particular train of thought persisted in, be it good or bad, cannot fail to produce its results on the character and circumstances. A woman cannot directly choose her circumstances, but she can choose her thoughts, and so indirectly, yet surely, shape her circumstances. Nature helps every woman to the gratification of her thoughts, which they most encourage, and opportunities are presented, which will most speedily bring to the surface both the good and the evil thoughts. Let a woman cease from her sinful thoughts, and the entire world will soften towards her, and be ready to help her. Let her put away her weakly and sickly thoughts and the opportunities will spring up on every hand to aid her strong resolve. Let her encourage good thoughts, and no hard fate shall bind her down to wretchedness and shame. The world is your kaleidoscope, and the varying combinations of colors, which at every succeeding moment it presents to you, are the exquisitely adjusted pictures of your ever-moving thoughts.

> You will be what you will to be;
> Let failure find its false content
> In that poor word, "environment,"
> But spirit scorns it, and is free.
>
> It masters time, it conquers space,
> It cows that boastful trickster, Chance,
> And bids the tyrant Circumstance
> Uncrown, and fill a servant's place.

The human will, that force unseen,
The offspring of deathless Soul,
Can hew a way to any goal,
Though walls of granite intervene.

Be not impatient in delay,
But wait as one who understands;
When spirit rises and commands,
The gods are ready to obey.

CHAPTER 3

EFFECTS OF THOUGHTS ON HEALTH AND BODY

The body is the servant of the mind. It obeys the operations of the mind, whether they be deliberately chosen or automatically expressed. At the bidding of unlawful thoughts the body sinks rapidly into disease and decay; at the command of glad and beautiful thoughts it becomes clothed with youthfulness and beauty.

Disease and health, like circumstances, are rooted in thought. Sickly thoughts will express themselves through a sickly body. Thoughts of fear have been known to kill a person as speedily as a bullet and they are continually killing thousands of people just as surely, though less rapidly.

The people who live in fear of disease are the people who get it. Anxiety quickly demoralizes the whole body, and lays it open to the entrance of disease; while impure thoughts, even if not physically indulged, will sooner shatter the nervous system.

Strong, pure, and happy thoughts build up the body in vigor and grace. The body is a delicate and plastic instrument, which responds readily to the thoughts by which it is impressed, and habits of thought will produce their own effects, good or bad, upon it.

Men and women will continue to have impure and

poisoned blood, so long as they propagate unclean thoughts. Out of a clean heart comes a clean life and a clean body. Out of a defiled mind comes a defiled life and a corrupt body. Thought is the source of action, life, and manifestation; make the fountain pure, and all will be pure. Change of diet will not help a person who will not change their thoughts. When a person makes their thoughts pure, they no longer desire impure food.

Clean thoughts make clean habits. The so-called saint who does not wash his body is not a saint. The person who has strengthened and purified their thoughts does not need to consider the malicious germ.

If you would perfect your body, guard your mind. If you would renew your body, beautify your mind. Thoughts of malice, envy, disappointment, and despondency, rob the body of its health and grace. A sour face does not come by chance; it is made by sour thoughts. Wrinkles that mar are drawn by folly, passion, and pride. I know a woman of ninety-six who has the bright, innocent face of a girl. I know a man, well under middle age, whose face is drawn into inharmonious contours. The one is the result of a sweet and sunny disposition; the other is the outcome of passion and discontent.

As you cannot have a sweet and wholesome abode unless you admit the air and sunshine freely into your rooms, so a strong body and a bright, happy, or serene countenance can only result from the free admittance into the mind of thoughts of joy and goodwill and serenity. On the faces of the aged there are wrinkles made by sympathy, others by strong and pure thought, and others are carved by passion. Who cannot distinguish them? With those who have lived righteously, age is calm, peaceful, and softly mellowed, like the setting sun.

I have recently seen a philosopher on his deathbed. He was not old except in years. He died as sweetly and peacefully as he had lived. There is no physician like cheerful thought for dissipating the ills of the body; there is no comforter to compare with goodwill for dispersing the shadows of grief and sorrow. To live continually in thoughts of ill will, cynicism, suspicion, and envy, is to be confined in a self-made prison hole. But to think well of all, to be cheerful with all, to patiently learn to find the good in all such unselfish thoughts are the very portals of heaven; and to dwell day by day in thoughts of peace toward every creature will bring abounding peace to their possessor.

CHAPTER 4

THOUGHT AND PURPOSE

Until thought is linked with purpose, there is no intelligent accomplishment. With the majority, the bark of thought is allowed to "drift" upon the ocean of life. Aimlessness is a vice, and such drifting must not continue for the woman who would steer clear of catastrophe and destruction. They who have no central purpose in their lives become an easy prey to petty worries, fears, troubles, and self-pity. All of which are indications of weakness, which lead, just as surely as deliberately planned sins (though by a different route), to failure, unhappiness, and loss, for weakness cannot persist in a power-evolving universe.

A woman should conceive of a legitimate purpose in her heart, and set out to accomplish it. A woman should make this purpose the centralizing point of her thoughts. It may take the form of a spiritual ideal, or it may be a worldly object, according to her nature at the time being. Whichever it is, she should steadily focus her thought forces upon the object she has set before her.

This woman should make this purpose her supreme duty and should devote herself to its attainment, not allowing her thoughts to wander away into ephemeral fancies, longings, and imaginings.

This is the royal road to self-control and true concentration of thought. Even if she fails again and again to accomplish her purpose—as she must until weakness is overcome—the strength of character gained will be the measure of her true success, and this will form a new starting point for future power and triumph.

Those who are not prepared for the apprehension of a great purpose should fix their thoughts upon the faultless performance of their duty, no matter how insignificant their task may appear. Only in this way can the thoughts be gathered and focused, and resolution and energy be developed. Once this is done, there is nothing that may not be accomplished. The weakest soul knowing its own weakness, and believing this truth—that strength can only be developed by effort and practice—will, thus believing, at once begin to exert itself. And, adding effort to effort, patience to patience, and strength to strength, will never cease to develop and will at last grow divinely strong.

As the physically weak woman can make herself strong by careful and patient training, so the woman of weak thoughts can make herself strong through the exercising of right thinking. To put away aimlessness and weakness and to begin to think with purpose is to enter the ranks of those strong ones who only recognize failure as one of the pathways to attainment; who make all conditions serve them, and who think strongly, attempt fearlessly, and accomplish masterfully. Having conceived of her purpose, a woman should mentally mark out a straight pathway to its achievement, looking neither to the right, nor the left. Doubts and fears should be rigorously excluded. They are disintegrating elements that break up the straight line of effort, rendering it crooked, ineffectual, and useless. Thoughts of doubt and fear can never accomplish anything. They always lead to failure.

Purpose, energy, power to do, and all strong thoughts cease when doubt and fear creep in. The will to do springs from the knowledge that we can do. Doubt and fear are the great enemies of knowledge, and the woman who encourages them, who does not slay them, thwarts herself at every step. The woman who has conquered doubt and fear has conquered failure. Her every thought is allied with power and all difficulties are bravely met and overcome. Her purposes are seasonably planted, and they bloom and bring forth fruit that does not fall prematurely to the ground. Thought allied fearlessly to purpose becomes creative force: the woman who knows this is ready to become something higher and stronger than a bundle of wavering thoughts and fluctuating sensations. The woman who does this has become the conscious and intelligent wielder of her mental powers.

CHAPTER 5

THE THOUGHT-FACTOR IN ACHIEVEMENT

All that a man achieves and all that he fails to achieve is the direct result of his own thoughts. In a justly ordered universe, where loss of equipoise would mean total destruction, individual responsibility must be absolute. A man's weakness and strength, purity and impurity, are his own and not another man's. They are brought about by himself and not by another; and they can only be altered by himself, never by another.

A man's condition is also his own, and not another man's. His sufferings and his happiness are evolved from within. As a man thinks, so is he; as he continues to think, so he remains.

A strong man cannot help a weaker, unless that weaker is willing to be helped. And even then, the weak people must become strong of themselves. They must, by their own efforts, develop the strength, which they admire in another. No one but a man himself can alter his condition.

It has been usual for people to think and to say, "Many people are slaves because one is an oppressor; let us hate the oppressor!" But there is amongst an increasing few a tendency to reverse this judgment and to say, "One man is an oppressor because many are slaves; let us despise the slaves." The truth is that oppressor and slaves are cooperators in ignorance, and while seeming to afflict each other, are in reality, afflicting themselves. A perfect knowledge perceives the action of law in the weakness of the oppressed and the misapplied power of the oppressor. A perfect love, seeing the suffering that both states entail, condemns neither; a perfect compassion embraces both oppressor and oppressed.

A man who has conquered weakness and has pushed away all selfish thoughts belongs neither to oppressor nor oppressed. He is free. A man can only rise, conquer, and achieve by lifting up his thoughts. He can only remain weak, abject, and miserable by refusing to lift up his thoughts.

Before a man can achieve anything, even in worldly things, he must lift his thoughts above slavish animal indulgence. He may not, in order to succeed, give up all bestial thoughts and selfishness necessarily, but a portion of it must, at least, be sacrificed. A man whose first thought is bestial indulgence could neither think clearly nor plan methodically. He could not find and develop his latent resources, and would fail in any undertaking. Not having commenced to fully control his thoughts, he is not in a position to control affairs and to adopt serious responsibilities.

He is not fit to act independently and stand alone. He is limited only by the thoughts that he chooses. There can be neither progress nor achievement without sacrifice, and a man's worldly success will be by the measure that he sacrifice his confused animal thoughts, and fix his mind on the development of his plans, and the strengthening of his resolution and self-reliance.

The higher a man lifts his thoughts, the greater will be his success, and the more blessed and enduring will be his achievements. The universe does not favor the greedy, the dishonest, the vicious, although on the mere surface it sometimes may appear to do so. It helps the honest, the magnanimous, and the virtuous. All the great teachers of the ages have declared this in varying ways, and to prove it and to know it, a man has but to persist in making himself increasingly virtuous by lifting his thoughts.

Intellectual achievements are the result of thought consecrated to the search for knowledge or for the beautiful and true in nature. Such achievements may sometimes be connected with vanity and ambition, but they are not the outcome of those characteristics. They are the natural outgrowth of long and arduous effort, and of pure and unselfish thoughts. Spiritual achievements are the consummation of holy aspirations. A man who lives constantly in the conception of noble and lofty thoughts, who dwells upon all that is pure and selfless will, as surely as the sun reaches its zenith and the moon its full, become wise and noble in character and rise into a position of influence and blessedness.

Achievement of any kind is the crown of effort and thought. By the aid of self-control, resolution, purity, righteousness, and well-directed thought, a man ascends. By the aid of bestial thoughts, indolence, impurity, corruption, and confusion of thought, a man descends. A man may rise to high success in the world, even to lofty attitudes in the spiritual realm, and again descend into weakness and wretchedness by allowing arrogant, selfish, and corrupt thoughts to take possession of him.

Victories attained by right thought can be maintained only by watchfulness. Many give way when success is assured, and rapidly fall back into failure. All achievements, whether in the business, intellectual, or spiritual world, are the result of definitely directed thought. They are governed by the same law and are of the same method. The only difference lies in the object of attainment. A man who would accomplish little need sacrifice little; a man who would achieve much must sacrifice much. A man who would attain highly must sacrifice greatly.

CHAPTER 6

VISIONS AND IDEALS

The dreamers are the saviors of the world. As the visible world is sustained by the invisible, so people, through all their trials and sins and sordid vocations are nourished by the beautiful visions of their solitary dreamers.

Humanity cannot forget its dreamers; it cannot let their ideals fade and die; it lives in them; it knows them as the realities which it shall one day see and know. Composer, sculptor, painter, poet, prophet, sage—these are the makers of the after-world, the architects of heaven. The world is beautiful because they have lived. Without them, laboring humanity would perish.

A person who cherishes a beautiful vision, a lofty ideal in his or her heart, will one day realize it. Columbus cherished a vision of another world and he discovered it. Copernicus fostered the vision of a multiplicity of worlds and a wider universe, and he revealed it. Buddha beheld the vision of a spiritual world of stainless beauty and perfect peace, and he entered into it. Cherish your visions; cherish your ideals. Cherish the music that stirs in your heart, the beauty that forms in your mind, and the loveliness that drapes your purest thoughts. For out of them will grow all delightful conditions, all heavenly environments; of these, if you but remain true to them, your world will at last be built.

To desire is to obtain; to aspire is to achieve. Shall a person's basest desires receive the fullest measure of gratification, and their purest aspirations starve for lack of sustenance? Such is not the Law. Such a condition can never obtain "Ask and receive." Dream lofty dreams, and as you dream, so shall you become. Your vision is the promise of what you shall one day be; your ideal is the prophecy of what you shall at last unveil.

The greatest achievement was at first and for a time a dream. The oak sleeps in the acorn; the bird waits in the egg. And in the highest vision of a soul, a waking angel stirs. Dreams are the seedlings of realities. Your circumstances may be uncongenial, but they shall not remain so if you only perceive an ideal and strive to reach it. You cannot travel within and stand still without.

Here is a youth hard pressed by poverty and labor; confined long hours in an unhealthy workshop; unschooled and lacking all the arts of refinement. But he dreams of better things. He thinks of intelligence or refinement, of grace and beauty. He conceives of, mentally builds up, an ideal condition of life. The wider liberty and a larger scope takes possession of him; unrest urges him to action, and he uses all his spare time and means, small as they are, to the development of his latent powers and resources.

Very soon, so altered has his mind become that the workshop can no longer hold him. It has become so out of harmony with his mind-set that it falls out of his life as a garment is cast aside. And with the growth of opportunities that fit the scope of his expanding powers, he passes out of it altogether.

Years later, we see this youth as an adult. We find him a master of certain forces of the mind that he wields with worldwide influence and almost unequaled power. In his hands he holds the cords of gigantic responsibilities; he speaks and lives are changed; people hang upon his words and remold their characters. And like the Sun, he becomes the fixed and luminous center around which innumerable destinies revolve. He has realized the vision of his youth. He has become one with his ideal.

And you, too, will realize the vision (not just the idle wish) of your heart, be it base or beautiful or a mixture of both for you will always gravitate toward that which you secretly love most. Into your hands will be placed the exact results of your own thoughts. You will receive that which you earn—no more, no less. Whatever your present environment may be, you will fall, remain, or rise with your thoughts, your vision, your ideal. You will become as small as your controlling desire, as great as your dominant aspiration.

The thoughtless, the ignorant, and the indolent, seeing only the apparent effects of things and not the things themselves, talk of luck, of fortune, and chance. Seeing a man grow rich, they say, "How lucky he is!" Observing another becoming intellectually skilled, they exclaim, "How highly favored he is!" And noting the saintly character and wide influence of another, they remark, "How chance helps her at every turn!"

They do not see the trials and failures and struggles that these people have encountered in order to gain their experience. They have no knowledge of the sacrifices they have made, of the undaunted efforts they have put forth, of the faith they have exercised so that they might overcome the apparently insurmountable and realize the vision of their hearts. They do not know the darkness and the heartaches; they only see the light and joy, and call it "luck." They do not see the long, arduous journey, but only behold the pleasant goal and call it "good fortune." They do not understand the process, but only perceive the result, and call it "chance."

In all human affairs there are efforts, and there are results. The strength of the effort is the measure of the result. Chance is not. Gifts, powers, material, intellectual, and spiritual possessions are the fruits of effort. They are thoughts completed, objectives accomplished, visions realized. The vision that you glorify in your mind, the ideal that you enthrone in your heart, by this you will build your life; by this you will become.

CHAPTER 7

SERENITY

Calmness of mind is one of the beautiful jewels of wisdom. It is the result of long and patient effort in self-control. Its presence is an indication of ripened experience, and of a more than an ordinary knowledge of the laws and operations of thought.

A man becomes calm in the measure that he understands himself as an evolving being. For such knowledge necessitates the understanding of others as the result of thought, and as he develops a right understanding, and sees ever more clearly the internal relations of things by the action of cause and effect, he ceases to fuss, fume, worry, and grieve. He remains poised, steadfast, and serene.

The calm man, having learned how to govern himself, knows how to adapt himself to others. And they, in turn, reverence his spiritual strength. They feel that they can learn from this calm person and rely upon him. The more tranquil a man becomes, the greater is his success, his influence, and his power for good. Even the ordinary trader will find his business prosperity increase as he develops a greater self-control and equanimity, for people will always prefer to deal with a person whose demeanor is equitable.

The strong, calm person is always loved and revered. That person is like a shade-giving tree in a thirsty land, or a sheltering rock in a storm. Who does not love a tranquil heart, a sweet-tempered, balanced life? It does not matter whether it rains or shines, or what changes come to those who possess these blessings, for this person is always serene and calm.

That exquisite poise of character that we call serenity is the last lesson of culture. It is the flowering of life, the fruitage of the soul. It is precious as wisdom and more desirable than fine gold. How insignificant mere money-seeking looks in comparison with a serene life. A life that dwells in the ocean of truth, beneath the waves, beyond the reach of the tempests, in the Eternal Calm!

How many people we know who sour their lives, who ruin all that is sweet and beautiful by explosive tempers, which destroy their poise of character and make bad blood! It is a question whether the great majority of people do not ruin their lives and mar their happiness by lack of self-control. How few people we meet in life who are well-balanced, who have that exquisite poise which is characteristic of the finished character!

Yes, humanity surges with uncontrolled passion, is tumultuous with ungoverned grief, is blown about by anxiety and doubt. Only the wise person, whose thoughts are controlled and purified, makes the winds and the storms of the soul obey them.

Tempest-tossed souls, wherever you may be, under whatever conditions you may live, know this: in the ocean of life, the isles of blessedness are smiling and the sunny shore of your ideal awaits your coming. Keep your hands firmly upon the helm of thought. In the core of your soul reclines the commanding Master; your master does but sleep. Awake your master. Self-control is strength. Right thought is mastery. Calmness is power. Say unto your heart, "Peace. Be still!"

LADIES AND GENTLEMEN,
INTRODUCING . . .

THE ONE, THE ONLY . . .

P.T. BARNUM
A BIOGRAPHY

P.T. Barnum was the quintessential entrepreneur. From humble beginnings, he rose to unbelievable wealth and prominence by giving the people of the world what they wanted then and still crave today—amusement.

Born on July 5, 1810 in Bethel, Connecticut, Phineas Taylor Barnum was named after his maternal grandfather, Phineas Taylor. Shortly after Barnum's birth, in appreciation of having his grandson named after him, Grandfather Taylor presented to his grandchild the deed to a tract of land outside Bethel, called "Ivy Island." At that age, the deed obviously meant nothing to Barnum, but as he grew older, his family members and the townspeople of Bethel repeatedly reminded young Barnum that Ivy Island was one of the most beautiful tracts of land in all of Connecticut.

Barnum naturally used this information to the best of his ability and would constantly remind everyone that he was "the richest child in Bethel." Finally, at the age of 12, Barnum set out to see his beautiful Ivy Island himself. When he finally arrived, he found that it was all a joke— Ivy Island was nothing but a swamp. Upon his return home, his family and fellow townspeople laughed about this little joke for a long time.

Now today, that would seem to be cruel, but back in Barnum's day, practical jokes were a common occurrence. Barnum himself in his autobiography, *Struggles and Triumphs or Forty Years' Recollections of P.T. Barnum*, recounts the episode with humor. For Barnum, it was the beginning of a life of practical jokes, exaggerations, and humbugs. It would also be the driving force for his lifelong quest for respect—an attribute that, even after his death, eluded him.

However, drive and determination were qualities that Barnum did possess and which he held onto all of his life. Barnum always felt that he was "destined to appear before the public in the character of a showman," and strangely enough, Ivy Island would help him begin his journey.

Around 1841, the American Museum—one of the first museums in the country—was up for sale. Thirty-one-year-old Barnum knew that if he could purchase the American Museum, he would be on his way to fulfilling his destiny as a showman. However, the owner wanted cash and Barnum was financially strapped. He decided to talk to the owner about his desire to recreate the Museum into a showpiece for the world. Impressed by Barnum's vision, energy, and commitment, the owner agreed to set up a payment schedule instead of a lump sum—with one caveat. That caveat was that the owner would need some form of security to insure the loan. "Perhaps," the owner suggested, "a piece of unencumbered land." Barnum quickly suggested Ivy Island. The owner agreed. Barnum got the museum and, to his credit, paid off the loan quickly.

As the proprietor of the Barnum Museum, Barnum began to school himself in the ways of business and promotion. Those early "struggles and triumphs" developed for Barnum not only the skills of a master showman, but also the business acumen that would serve him the rest of his life. He became an expert in advertising, marketing, sales, and public relations.

"Advertising is like learning; a little is a dangerous thing," was one of Barnum's favorite mottoes to which he faithfully adhered the rest of his life. Barnum was the first to use searchlights, banners, fireworks, parades, games, contests, bands, leaflets, brochures, press releases, sandwich boards, and publicity stunts as various means to increase attention and traffic to his museum.

Barnum spared no expense in drawing excitement, attention, and interest to anything that he ever did, because he knew that good advertising and promotion would always deliver paying customers.

When the paying customers did arrive, they were always overwhelmed by what they saw. Barnum gave his customers their money's worth. There was a lot to see in Barnum's Museum—so much, that his customers began to bring lunches and spend all day at the attraction. However, this activity soon became a problem. New customers couldn't get in to the Museum, because the old customers were slow to leave.

The ever-resourceful Barnum took care of this little problem the best way he knew how, by developing a new "exhibit" that would "thin out the crowd." He made elaborate signs that stated, "This way to the Egress," and the customers duly followed. However, it wasn't until the customers ended up back on the street that they realized that the word "egress" is another word for "exit." Regardless of this little joke, and the many others that were played on his customers, the American Museum grew to become one of the premier attractions, drawing more people in its day, comparatively speaking, than Disneyland does today.

Many of the exhibits at Barnum's Museum were phenomenal pieces of history. Some were full of human interest such as Chang and Eng (the famous Siamese twins), while others were pure "humbug." For example, Barnum exhibited Joice Heth who was (falsely) believed to be 161 years old and the nurse to George Washington. He also exhibited the Fejee Mermaid, which, in reality, was the top half of a deceased and decayed monkey sewed to the bottom half of a fish.

Barnum's Museum brought fame and wealth to its proprietor, and regardless of the humbugs, people came to be amused. And amuse them he did. For a while, Barnum even called himself the "Prince of Humbugs," but he eventually grew tired of being associated with "something designed to deceive and mislead." Barnum knew that he needed to find an attraction that would erase the word "humbug" from people's minds and firmly etch the word "respect" in its place.

Enter Tom Thumb, only 31 inches tall, whose childlike appearance was only surpassed by his amazing acting and imitative ability. Barnum worked with Thumb to develop and hone his performance skills, and together they made an incredible team. Thumb and Barnum traveled the world gaining the attention and admiration of Kings, Queens, and Presidents, as well as tumultuous amounts of favorable press. Barnum was—in his mind—one step closer to achieving his desire for respect.

Around 1851, Barnum "relished a higher grade of amusement" and wanted to provide the same to the world. Barnum wanted an attraction that was already established, highly respected, and, with his careful guidance, would make him more money. He found his attraction in Jenny Lind, the "Swedish Nightingale." Jenny Lind was an opera singer, a soprano with "the voice of an angel." Barnum turned Lind into the world's first "superstar."

Because of Barnum's acumen at garnering publicity and his ingenious advertising and marketing skills, before Lind set foot on American soil, her performances were sold out. She, along with Barnum, would reach the pinnacle of show business success. America and England were completely taken under by her spell—or perhaps it was *Barnum's* spell. Songs, poems, and books were written about Lind. Her name appeared on mugs, dishes, charms, and hundreds of other items and souvenirs.

As Thumb did before her, Lind became very wealthy, and of course, Barnum did incredibly well financially himself. Yet, there was another reason why Barnum was especially proud of his success with Lind. Lind was a real star— an opera star. Barnum took a highly respected opera singer and turned her into the greatest sensation of that period. Again, in Barnum's mind, he was moving closer and closer to obtaining his elusive goal.

Barnum had made millions and had acquired what he felt was a respectable place in society. He had an extravagant home and the very best carriage. In fact, Barnum had the very best of everything, and he never hesitated to show it off. He invested in others' businesses, purchased art, and acquired real estate. About real estate Barnum said, "It is the investment that keeps growing, while the owner is asleep." His lavish lifestyle continued uninterrupted, until Barnum made the wrong investment in the wrong company. He invested in a number of clock-making companies—something he knew nothing about—and became bankrupt. P.T. Barnum lost everything.

This blow would have crushed most people, but not Barnum. He decided that he would repay his debts and become, again, financially stable and, hopefully, respected. (Incidentally, Mark Twain also made a bad investment and lost everything. Twain, like Barnum, would eventually repay his debt and successfully emerge from bankruptcy.) Not knowing which way to turn to recoup his losses, Barnum was encouraged by his friends to develop a lecture on how to make money. Barnum was unsure if this was a wise thing to do, considering he was now bankrupt. In fact, he thought that an apt title would be *The Art of Money-Losing*. However, his friends reminded him that in order to lose money, one had to have made money in the first place.

With that in mind, in 1858, Barnum developed a lecture that he called *The Art of Money-Getting*. In it, Barnum shared his knowledge of business, success, and happiness. And like many motivational speakers of his time and ours, what Barnum stated in his lecture regarding "what one should do," Barnum "sometimes didn't." However, Barnum did practice most of what he preached. He began to tour around the country and England with this lecture. Speaking primarily in large halls, universities, and business colleges, those who paid to hear what he had to say were rewarded with usable information that is still relevant and true today. It is historically correct to state that many people of his day, and since then, have become millionaires by what they learned from Barnum's *The Art of Money-Getting*.

The Art of Money-Getting allowed Barnum to pay back his debts and recoup his worth. In fact, after he emerged from bankruptcy, he found his speech was a "real money-maker" and continued to deliver it for many years. Barnum always liked to make money. Yet, the bankruptcy had slightly altered his mindset; he found that he no longer needed all of the "extravagant trappings of success." He learned to be more patient, more giving, and more humble. Even with these changes, one thought remained constant in Barnum's mind—he still yearned for respect.

Over the years, Barnum had been slowly making the transformation from his self-imposed title as the "Prince of Humbugs" to the new moniker of the "Genial Showman." As his income grew, so did his later accomplishments, most noticeably his recreation and reorganization of the circus—The Greatest Show on Earth—a monumental undertaking that Barnum accomplished while in his 60s.

Barnum was a man who was usually in good health and upbeat in spirit. A heavy cigar smoker and a big eater, Barnum lived life to the fullest. He credited his success to "energy, perseverance, attention to business detail, and tact." A spiritual man, Barnum always gave credit to God. One of his favorite sayings was "All praise to Him for permitting me always to look on the bright side of things," and despite of all of his struggles and triumphs, Barnum always kept a positive outlook and shunned negativity.

Barnum's contributions to the world of amusement are immense. His contributions to the world of advertising, public relations, marketing, and salesmanship are also vast and impressive. His success with the American Museum, Tom Thumb, Jenny Lind, the circus, and later

Jumbo the elephant, allowed Barnum to hone his skills as a showman and businessman. Those whose business it is to capture the minds and emotions of potential buyers are still using many of his business and promotional ideas today.

When Barnum died on April 7, 1891, he left behind a staggering fortune. He accomplished so much, yet ironically, outside of the circus, Barnum is primarily remembered for a statement that he never made. Today, when you mention the name "Barnum," people respond with, "He's the guy who said, 'There's a sucker born every minute.'" Barnum was too astute of a businessperson to ever make that sort of statement. It was actually said by one of his competitors who was jealous of Barnum. Yet, that negative statement has been permanently affixed in the minds of people throughout the world. Even in death, his ceaseless quest for "respect" is still just out of reach.

Barnum did say, "Every crowd has a silver lining," and that statement has been proven to be true. For whenever people get together to go to a concert, an opera, a museum, an aquarium, or any type of event that promises to be amusing or entertaining, there is always money to be made. And for those who make that money and for those who "enjoy the show," a silent thank you should be sent toward heaven for the man who helped to make the profits and the amusement possible. That man is P.T. Barnum.

I have read Barnum's biography and *The Art of Money-Getting* countless times. With every reading, I learn something new. In my humble opinion, **The Art of Money-Getting is a bible for business success.**

It is hoped that this edition of P.T. Barnum's *The Art of Money-Getting* brings you enjoyment . . . and profit.

For more information on the life of P.T. Barnum, visit: http://www.barnum-museum.org/. Barnum's American Museum is still in existence today and is located at 820 Main Street in Bridgeport, CT. It's operated by a group of dedicated and talented people. Call (203) 331-1104.

Other writings and reference:

Barnum, P.T., *Struggles and Triumphs or Forty Years' Recollections of P.T. Barnum*, New York, Warren, Johnson & Company, 1873.

Wallace, Irving, *The Fabulous Showman—The Life and Times of P.T. Barnum*, New York, Alfred A. Knopf, Inc., 1959.

Harris, Neil, *Humbug: The Art of P.T. Barnum*, Boston, Little, Brown and Company, 1973.

Saxon, A.H., *P.T. Barnum: The Legend and the Man*, New York, Columbia University Press, 1989.

Saxon, A.H., *Selected Letters of P.T. Barnum*, New York, Columbia University Press, 1983.

To hear a recording of Barnum's voice, one of the first made by Thomas Edison, go to: www.historybuff.com/media/historicvoices.

THE ART OF MONEY-GETTING

BY P.T. BARNUM

THE ART OF MONEY-GETTING

In the United States, where we have more land than people, it is not at all difficult for people in good health to make money. In this comparatively new field, there are so many avenues of success open, so many vocations which are not crowded, that any person of either sex who is willing, at least for the time being, to engage in any respectable occupation that appears, may find lucrative employment.

Those who really desire to attain an independence have only to set their minds upon it, and adopt the proper means, as they do in regard to any other object they wish to accomplish, and the thing is easily done. However easy it may be to make money, I have no doubt many of my listeners will agree it is the most difficult thing in the world to keep it. The road to wealth is, as Dr. Franklin truly says, "as plain as the road to the mill." It consists simply of expending less than we earn; that seems to be a very simple problem. Mr. Micawber, one of those happy creations of the genial Dickens, puts the case in a strong light when he says that to have an income of twenty pounds per annum, and spend twenty pounds and sixpence, is to be the most miserable of men; whereas, to have an income of only twenty pounds, and spend but nineteen pounds and sixpence is to be the happiest of mortals.

Many of my readers may say, "We understand this; this is economy, and we know economy is wealth; we know we can't eat our cake and keep it also." Yet, I beg to say that perhaps more cases of failure arise from mistakes on this point than almost any other. The fact is that many people think they understand economy, when they really do not.

True economy is misapprehended, and people go through life without properly comprehending what that principle is. One says, "I have an income of so much and here is my neighbor who has the same; yet every year he gets something ahead and I fall short; why is it? I know all about economy." He thinks he does, but he does not. There are many who think that economy consists in saving cheese-parings and candle-ends, in cutting off two pence from the laundress's bill and doing all sorts of little, mean, dirty things. Economy is not meanness. The misfortune is also that this class of persons let their economy apply in only one direction. They fancy they are so wonderfully economical in saving a halfpenny, where they ought to spend two pence, that they think they can afford to squander in other directions.

A few years ago, before kerosene oil was discovered or thought of, one might stop overnight at almost any farmer's house in the agricultural districts and get a very good supper, but after supper he might attempt to read in the sitting room, and would find it impossible with the inefficient light of one candle. The hostess, seeing his dilemma, would say, "It is rather difficult to read here evenings. The proverb says 'you must have a ship at sea in order to be able to burn two candles at once.' We never have an extra candle except on extra occasions." These extra occasions occur, perhaps, twice a year. In this way, the good woman saves five, six, or ten dollars in that time; but the information, which might be derived from having the extra light, would, of course, far outweigh a ton of candles.

However, the trouble does not end here. Feeling that she is so economical in tallow candles, she thinks she can afford to frequently go to the village and spend twenty or thirty dollars for ribbons and ruffles, many of which are not necessary. This false economy may frequently be seen in men of business, and in those instances it often runs to writing paper. You find good businessmen who save all the old envelopes and scraps, and would not tear a new sheet of paper if they could avoid it for the world. This is all very well; they may in this way save five or ten dollars a year; but being so economical (only in note paper), they think they can afford to waste time, to have expensive parties, and to drive their carriages.

This is an illustration of Dr. Franklin's "saving at the spigot and wasting at the bung-hole" or "penny wise and pound foolish." *Punch* in speaking of this "one idea" class of people says, "They are like the man who bought a penny herring for his family's dinner and then hired a coach and four to take it home." I never knew a man to succeed by practicing this kind of economy.

True economy consists in always making the income exceed the outgo. Wear the old clothes a little longer, if necessary; dispense with the new pair of gloves; mend the old dress; live on plainer food, if need be; so that, under all circumstances, unless some unforeseen accident occurs, there will be a margin in favor of the income. A penny here and a dollar there, placed at interest, goes on accumulating, and in this way, the desired result is attained. It requires some training, perhaps, to accomplish this economy, but when once used to it, you will find there is more satisfaction in rational saving, than in irrational spending.

Here is a recipe that I have found to work as an excellent cure for extravagance and especially for mistaken economy: When you find that you have no surplus at the end of the year, and yet have a good income, I advise you to take a few sheets of paper, form them into a book, and mark down every item of expenditure. Post it every day or week in two columns, one headed "necessaries" or even "comforts," and the other headed "luxuries," and you will find that the latter column will be double, treble, and frequently be ten times greater than the former.

The real comforts of life cost but a small portion of what most of us can earn. Dr. Franklin says, "It is the eyes of others and not our own eyes which ruin us. If all the world were blind, except myself, I should not care for fine clothes or furniture." It is the fear of what Mrs. Grundy may say that keeps the noses of many worthy families to the grindstone. In America, many persons like to repeat "we are all free and equal," but it is a great mistake, in more senses than one.

That we are born "free and equal" is a glorious truth in one sense, yet we are not all born equally rich, and we never shall be. One may say, "There is a man who has an income of fifty thousand dollars per annum, while I have but one thousand dollars; I knew that fellow when he was poor like myself. Now, he is rich and thinks he is better than I am. I will show him that I am as good as he is. I will go and buy a horse and buggy. No, I cannot do that, but I will go and hire one and ride this afternoon on the same road that he does, and thus prove to him that I am as good as he is."

My friend, you need not take that trouble; you can easily prove that you are "as good as he is"; you have only to behave as well as he does—but you cannot make anybody believe that you are rich as he is. Besides, if you put on these "airs," waste your time and spend your money, your poor wife will be obliged to scrub her fingers off at home. She will be forced to buy her tea two ounces at a time and everything else in proportion, in order that you may keep up "appearances," and, after all, deceive nobody.

On the other hand, Mrs. Smith may say that her next door neighbor married Johnson for his money, and "everybody says so." She has a nice one thousand dollar camel's hair shawl, and she will make Smith get her an imitation one, and she will sit in a pew right next to her neighbor in church, in order to prove that she is her equal.

My good woman, you will not get ahead in the world, if your vanity and envy thus take the lead. In this country, where we believe the majority ought to rule, we ignore that principle—in regard to fashion—and let a handful of people, calling themselves aristocracy, run up a false standard of perfection. In endeavoring to rise to that standard, we constantly keep ourselves poor, all the time digging away for the sake of outside appearances. How much wiser to be a "law unto ourselves" and say, "We will regulate our outgo by our income, and lay up something for a rainy day."

People ought to be as sensible on the subject of money-getting as on any other subject. Like causes produce like effects. You cannot accumulate a fortune by taking the road that leads to poverty. It needs no prophet to tell us that those who live fully up to their means, without any thought of a reverse in this life, can never attain a pecuniary independence.

Men and women accustomed to gratify every whim and fancy will find it hard, at first, to cut down their various unnecessary expenses. They will feel it a great self-denial to live in a smaller house than they have been accustomed to, with less expensive furniture, less company, less costly clothing, fewer servants, a less number of balls, parties, theater goings, carriage-ridings, pleasure excursions, cigar smokings, liquor drinkings, and other extravagances. But, after all, if they will try the plan of laying by a "nest-egg," or in other words, a small sum of money, at interest or judiciously invested in land, they will be surprised at the pleasure to be derived from constantly adding to their little "pile," as well as from all the economical habits which are engendered by this course.

The old suit of clothes, and the old bonnet and dress, will answer for another season; the Croton or spring water will taste better than champagne; a cold bath and a brisk walk will prove more exhilarating than a ride in the finest coach. A social chat, an evening's reading in the family circle, or an hour's play of "hunt the slipper" and "blind man's buff" will be far more pleasant than a fifty or five hundred dollar party, when the reflection on the difference in cost is indulged in by those who begin to know the pleasures of saving.

Thousands of men are kept poor and tens of thousands are made so, after they have acquired enough to support them well through life, in consequence of laying their plans of living on too broad a platform. Some families expend twenty thousand dollars per annum, and some much more, and would scarcely know how to live on less, while others secure more solid enjoyment frequently on a twentieth part of that amount.

Prosperity is a more severe ordeal than adversity, especially sudden prosperity. "Easy come, easy go," is an old and true proverb. A spirit of pride and vanity, when permitted to have full sway, is the undying worm that gnaws the very vitals of a man's worldly possessions, let them be small or great, hundreds or millions. Many persons, as they begin to prosper, immediately expand their ideas and commence expending for luxuries until, in a short time, their expenses swallow up their income, and they become ruined in their ridiculous attempts to keep up appearances and make a "sensation."

I know a gentleman of fortune who says that when he first began to prosper, his wife would have a new and elegant sofa. "That sofa" he says, "cost me thirty thousand dollars!" When the sofa reached the house, it was found necessary to get chairs to match; then side-boards, carpets and tables "to correspond" with them, and so on through the entire stock of furniture. Then, at last it was found that the house itself was quite too small and old-fashioned for the furniture, and a new one was built to correspond with the new purchases. "Thus," added my friend, "summing up an outlay of thirty thousand dollars, caused by that single sofa, and saddling on me, in the shape of servants, equipage, and the necessary expenses attendant upon keeping up a fine 'establishment,' a yearly outlay of eleven thousand dollars, and a tight pinch at that. Whereas ten years ago, we lived with much more real comfort, with much less care on as many hundreds." "The truth is," he continued, "that sofa would have brought me to inevitable bankruptcy, had not a most unexampled tide of prosperity kept me above it, and had I not checked the natural desire to claim bankruptcy."

The foundation of success in life is good health; that is the substructure of fortune; it is also the basis of happiness. A person cannot accumulate a fortune very well when he is sick. He or she has no ambition; no incentive; no force. Of course, there are those who have bad health and cannot help it; you cannot expect that such persons can accumulate wealth, but there are a great many in poor health who need not be so.

If, then, sound health is the foundation of success and happiness in life, how important it is that we should study the laws of health, which is but another expression for the laws of nature! The closer we keep to the laws of nature, the nearer we are to good health, and yet how many persons there are who pay no attention to natural laws, but absolutely transgress them, even against their own natural inclination. We ought to know that the "sin of ignorance" is never winked at, in regard to the violation of nature's laws; their infraction always brings the penalty.

A child may thrust its finger into the flames without knowing it will burn, and so suffers. Even repentance will not stop the smart. Many of our ancestors knew very little about the principle of ventilation. They did not know much about oxygen, whatever other "gin" they might have been acquainted with, and consequently, they built their houses with little seven-by-nine feet bedrooms, and these good old pious Puritans would lock themselves up in one of these cells, say their prayers and go to bed. In the morning, they would devoutly return thanks for the "preservation of their lives," during the night, and nobody had better reason to be thankful. Probably some big crack in the window or in the door let in a little fresh air, and thus saved them.

Many people knowingly violate the laws of nature against their better impulses, for the sake of fashion. For instance, there is one thing that nothing living, except a vile worm, ever naturally loved and that is tobacco. Yet, how many persons there are who deliberately train an unnatural appetite and overcome this implanted aversion for tobacco to such a degree that they get to love it. They have gotten hold of a poisonous, filthy weed; or rather, it takes a firm hold of them.

Here are married men who run about spitting tobacco juice on the carpet and floors, and sometimes even upon their wives besides. They do not kick their wives out of doors like drunken men, but their wives, I have no doubt, often wish they were outside of the house. Another perilous feature is that this artificial appetite, like jealousy, "grows by what it feeds on," when you love that which is unnatural, a stronger appetite is created for the hurtful thing than the natural desire for what is harmless.

There is an old proverb that says, "Habit is second nature." But an artificial habit is stronger than nature. Take for instance, an old tobacco chewer; his love for the "quid" is stronger than his love for any particular kind of food. He can give up roast beef easier than give up the weed.

Young lads regret that they are not men; they would like to go to bed boys and wake up men; and to accomplish this they copy the bad habits of their seniors. Little Tommy and Johnny see their fathers or uncles smoke a pipe, and they say, "If I could only do that, I would be a man too. Uncle John has gone out and left his pipe of tobacco, let us try it." They take a match, light it, and then puff away. "We will learn to smoke; do you like it Johnny?" That lad dolefully replies, "Not very much; it tastes bitter." Then, by and by, Johnny grows pale, but he persists and he soon offers up a sacrifice on the altar of fashion. Yet, the boys stick to it and persevere, until at last they conquer their natural appetites and become the victims of acquired tastes.

I speak "by the book," for I have noticed its effects on myself, having gone so far as to smoke ten or fifteen cigars a day, although I have not used the weed during the last fourteen years and never shall again. The more a man smokes, the more he craves smoking; the last cigar smoked simply excites the desire for another, and so on incessantly.

Take the tobacco chewer. In the morning, when he gets up, he puts a quid in his mouth and keeps it there all day, never taking it out, except to exchange it for a fresh one or when he is going to eat. Oh! Yes, at intervals during the day and evening, many a chewer takes out the quid and holds it in his hand long enough to take a drink, and then "pop"—it goes back again. This simply proves that the appetite for rum is even stronger than that for tobacco. When the tobacco chewer goes to your country seat and you show him your grapery, your fruit house, and the beauties of your garden, when you offer him some fresh, ripe fruit, and say, "My friend, I have got here the most delicious apples, pears, peaches, and apricots imported from Spain, France and Italy. Just see those luscious grapes! There is nothing more delicious nor more healthy than ripe fruit, so help yourself. I want to see you delight yourself with these things." He will roll the dear quid under his tongue and answer, "No, I thank you, I have got tobacco in my mouth." The noxious weed has narcotized his palate, and he has lost, in a great measure, the delicate and enviable taste for fruits.

This shows what expensive, useless and injurious habits men will get into. I speak from experience. I have smoked until I trembled like an aspen leaf, the blood rushed to my head, and I had a palpitation of the heart which I thought was heart disease, till I was almost killed with fright. When I consulted my physician, he said, "Break off tobacco using." I was not only injuring my health and spending a great deal of money, but I was setting a bad example. I obeyed his counsel. No young man in the world ever looked so beautiful as he thought he did, behind a fifteen-cent cigar or a meerschaum pipe!

These remarks apply with tenfold force to the use of intoxicating drinks. To make money requires a clear brain. A person has to see that two and two make four; this person must lay all his or her plans with reflection and forethought, and closely examine all the details and the ins and outs of business. No person can succeed in business, unless he or she has a brain to enable the laying of plans and the reason to guide in their execution. No matter how bountifully a person may be blessed with intelligence, if the brain is muddled and a person's judgment warped by intoxicating drinks, it is impossible to carry on business successfully.

How many good opportunities have passed, never to return, while a person was sipping a "social glass" with his or her friend? How many foolish bargains have been made under the influence of the "grape," which temporarily makes its victim think that he or she is rich? How many important chances have been put off until tomorrow, and then forever, because the wine cup has thrown the system into a state of lassitude, neutralizing the energies so essential to success in business?

Verily, "Wine is a mocker." The use of intoxicating drinks as a beverage is as much an infatuation as is the smoking of opium, and the former is quite as destructive to the success of the businessperson as the latter. It is an unmitigated evil, utterly indefensible in the light of philosophy, religion, or good sense. It is the parent of nearly every other evil in our country.

DON'T MISTAKE YOUR VOCATION

The safest plan, and the one most sure of success for the young man or woman starting in life, is to select the vocation which is most congenial to his or her tastes. Parents and guardians are often quite too negligent in regard to this. It is very common for a father to say, for example: "I have five boys. I will make Billy a clergyman, John a lawyer, Tom a doctor, and Dick a farmer." He then goes into town and looks about to see what he will do with Sammy. He returns home and says, "Sammy, I see watch-making is a nice, genteel business; I think I will make you a goldsmith." He does this, regardless of Sam's natural inclinations or genius.

We are all, no doubt, born for a wise purpose. There is as much diversity in our brains as in our countenances. Some are born natural mechanics, while some have great aversion to machinery. Let a dozen boys of ten years get together, and you will soon observe two or three are "whittling" out some ingenious device, working with locks or complicated machinery. When they were but five years old, their father could find no toy to please them like a puzzle. They are natural mechanics; but the other eight or nine boys have different aptitudes. I belong to the latter class; I never had the slightest love for mechanism. On the contrary, I have a sort of abhorrence for complicated machinery. I never had ingenuity enough to whittle a cider tap, so it would not leak. I never could make a pen that I could write with or understand the principle of a steam engine. If a man were to take such a boy as I was and attempt to make a watchmaker of him, the boy might, after an apprenticeship of five or seven years, be able to take apart and put together a watch. However, all through life he would be working uphill and seizing every excuse for leaving his work and idling away his time. Watch making is repulsive to him.

Unless a person enters upon the vocation intended for him or her by nature, and best suited to his or her peculiar genius, a person cannot succeed. I am glad to believe that the majority of persons do find their right vocation. Yet, we see many who have mistaken their calling, from the blacksmith up (or down) to the clergyman. You will see, for instance, that extraordinary linguist, the "learned blacksmith," who ought to have been a teacher of languages; and you may have seen lawyers, doctors and clergymen who were better fitted by nature for the anvil.

SELECT THE RIGHT LOCATION

After securing the right vocation, you must be careful to select the proper location. You may have been cut out for a hotel keeper, and they say it requires a genius to "know how to keep a hotel." You might conduct a hotel like clockwork and provide satisfactorily for five hundred guests every day. Yet, if you should locate your house in a small village where there is no railroad communication or public travel, the location would be your ruin. It is equally important that you do not commence business where there are already enough to meet all demands in the same occupation.

I remember a case that illustrates this subject. When I was in London in 1858, I was passing down Holborn with an English friend and came to the "penny shows." They had immense cartoons outside, portraying the wonderful curiosities to be seen "all for a penny." Being a little in the "show line" myself, I said, "Let us go in here."

We soon found ourselves in the presence of the illustrious showman, and he proved to be the sharpest man in that line I had ever met. He told us some extraordinary stories in reference to his "curiosities," which we could hardly believe, but thought it "better to believe it than look after the proof." He finally begged to call our attention to some wax statuary, and showed us some of the dirtiest and filthiest wax figures imaginable. They looked as if they had not seen water since the flood.

"What is there so wonderful about your statuary?" I asked.

"I beg you not to speak so satirically," he replied, "Sir, these are not Madam Tussaud's wax figures, all covered with gilt and tinsel and imitation diamonds, and copied from engravings and photographs. Mine, sir, were taken from life. Whenever you look upon one of those figures, you may consider that you are looking upon the living individual."

Glancing casually at them, I saw one labeled "Henry VIII," and—feeling a little curious—upon seeing that it looked like Calvin Edson, the living skeleton, I said: "Do you call that 'Henry, the Eighth?' "

He replied, "Certainly, sir; it was taken from life at Hampton Court, by special order of his majesty, on such a day."

He would have given the hour of the day, if I had insisted. I said, "Everybody knows that Henry VIII was a great stout old king, and that figure is lean and lank. What do you say to that?"

"Why," he replied, "you would be lean and lank yourself, if you sat there as long as he has."

There was no resisting such arguments. I said to my English friend, "Let us go out. Do not tell him who I am. I show the white feather; he beats me." He followed us to the door, and seeing the rabble in the street, he called out, "Ladies and Gentlemen, I beg to draw your attention to the respectable character of my visitors," pointing to us, as we walked away. I called upon him a couple of days after-wards, told him who I was, and said, "My friend, you are an excellent showman, but you have selected a bad location."

He replied, "This is true, sir. I feel that all my talents are thrown away, but what can I do?"

"You can go to America," I replied. "You can give full play to your faculties over there. You will find plenty of elbow-room in America. I will engage you for two years; after that, you will be able to go on your own account."

He accepted my offer and remained two years in my New York Museum. He then went to New Orleans and car-ried on a traveling show business during the summer. Today, he is worth sixty thousand dollars, simply because he selected the right vocation and also secured the proper location. The old proverb says, "Three moves are as bad as a fire," but when a man is in the fire, it matters but little how soon or how often he moves.

AVOID DEBT

Young men and women starting in life should avoid running into debt. There is scarcely anything that drags a person down like debt. It is a slavish position to get in, yet we find many young men and women, hardly out of their "teens" running in debt. He or she meets a friend and says, "Look at this! I have purchased these new clothes on cred-it." This young man or woman seems to look upon the clothes as so much given to them. And well, it frequently is so, but, if he or she succeeds in paying and then buys something else on credit again, this young person is adopt-ing a habit which will keep them in poverty through life.

Debt robs a person of self-respect and makes a person almost despise himself. Grunting and groaning and working for what they have eaten up or worn out, and now when they are called upon to pay up, they have nothing to show for their money. This is properly termed "working for a dead horse."

I do not speak of merchants buying and selling on credit, or of those who buy on credit in order to turn the purchase to a profit. The old Quaker said to his farmer son, "John, never buy on credit; but if thee buy on credit for anything, let it be for manure, because that will help thee pay it back again."

Mr. Beecher advised young men and women to get in debt, if they could to a small amount, in the purchase of land in the country districts. "If a young man or woman," he says, "will only get in debt for some land and then get married, these two things will keep them straight, or nothing will." This may be safe to a limited extent, but getting in debt for what you eat, drink, and wear is to be avoided. Some families have a foolish habit of getting credit at the stores, and thus frequently purchase many things which might have been dispensed with.

It is all very well to say, "I have been given credit for sixty days, and if I don't have the money the creditor will think nothing about it." There is no class of people in the world who have such good memories as creditors. When the sixty days run out, you will have to pay. If you do not pay, you will break your promise, and probably resort to a falsehood. You may make some excuse or get in debt elsewhere to pay it, but that only involves you the deeper.

A good-looking, lazy young fellow was the apprentice boy, Horatio. His employer said, "Horatio, did you ever see a snail?"

"I—think—I—have," he drawled out.

"You must have met him then, for I am sure you never

overtook one," said the boss. Your creditor will meet you or overtake you and say, "Now, my young friend, you agreed to pay me. You have not done it; you must pay me interest." You begin paying interest, and it commences working against you; it is a dead horse.

The creditor goes to bed at night and wakes up in the morning better off than when he retired to bed, because the money from your interest has increased during the night, but you grow poorer while you are sleeping, for the interest is accumulating against you.

Money is in some respects like fire—it is an excellent servant, but a terrible master. When you have it mastering you, when interest is constantly piling up against you, it will keep you down in the worst kind of slavery. However, let money work for you, and you have the most devoted servant in the world. There is nothing animate or inanimate that will work so faithfully as money when placed at interest, well secured. It works night and day, and in wet or dry weather.

I was born in the blue-law State of Connecticut, where the old Puritans had laws so rigid that it was said, "They fined a man for kissing his wife on Sunday." Yet, these rich old Puritans would have thousands of dollars at interest, and on Saturday night would be worth a certain amount. On Sunday, they would go to church and perform all the duties of a Christian. On waking up on Monday morning, they would find themselves considerably richer than the Saturday night previous, simply because their money placed at interest had worked faithfully for them all day Sunday, according to law!

Do not let it work against you. If you do there is no chance for success in life—so far as money is concerned. John Randolph, the eccentric Virginian, once exclaimed in

Congress, "Mr. Speaker, I have discovered the philosopher's stone: pay as you go." This is, indeed, nearer to the philosopher's stone than any alchemist has ever yet arrived.

PERSEVERE

When a person is in the right path, they must persevere. I speak of this because there are some people who are born tired, naturally lazy, and possessing no self-reliance and no perseverance. But they can cultivate these qualities.

As Davy Crockett said:
"This thing remember, when I am dead,
Be sure you are right, then go ahead."

It is this perseverance—this determination not to let the "horrors" or the "blues" take possession of you, so as to make you relax your energies in the struggle for independence—which you must cultivate. How many have almost reached the goal of their ambition, but losing faith in themselves, have relaxed their energies, and the golden prize has been lost forever. It is no doubt often true.

As Shakespeare said:
"There is a tide in the affairs of men,
Which taken at the flood, leads on to fortune."

If you hesitate, some bolder hand will stretch out before you and get the prize. Remember the proverb of Solomon, "He becometh poor that dealeth with a slack hand; but the hand of the diligent maketh rich."

Perseverance is sometimes just another word for self-reliance. Many people naturally look on the dark side of life and borrow trouble. They are born so. Then they ask for advice, and they will be governed by one wind and blown by another, and cannot rely upon themselves. Until you can get so that you can rely upon yourself, you need not expect to succeed. I have known men and women, personally, who have met with pecuniary reverses and absolutely committed suicide, because they thought they could never overcome their misfortune. But, I have known others who have met more serious financial difficulties and have bridged them over by simple perseverance, aided by a firm belief that they were doing justly, and that Providence would "overcome evil with good."

You will see this illustrated in any sphere of life.

Take two generals. Both understand military tactics; both are educated at West Point; if you please, both equally gifted; yet one, having this principle of perseverance, and the other lacking it, the former will succeed in his profession, while the latter will fail. One may hear the cry, "The enemy is coming, and they have got cannon."

"Got cannon?" says the hesitating general.

"Yes."

"Then halt every man," says the hesitating general.

He wants time to reflect; his hesitation is his ruin. The enemy passes unmolested or overwhelms him. While on the other hand, the general of pluck, perseverance, and self-reliance goes into battle with a will. And amid the clash of arms, the booming of cannon, the shrieks of the wounded, and the moans of the dying, you will see this man persevering, going on, cutting and slashing his way through with unwavering determination, inspiring his soldiers to deeds of fortitude, valor, and triumph.

WHATEVER YOU DO, DO IT WITH ALL YOUR MIGHT

Work at it, if necessary, early and late, in season and out of season, not leaving a stone unturned, and never deferring for a single hour that which can be done just as well *now*. The old proverb is full of truth and meaning, "Whatever is worth doing at all, is worth doing well." Many a person acquires a fortune by doing their business thoroughly, while their neighbor remains poor for life, because the neighbor only half does it.

Ambition, energy, industry, and perseverance are indispensable requisites for success in business. Fortune always favors the brave and never helps people who do not help themselves. It won't do to spend your time like Mr. Micawber, in waiting for something to "turn up." To such people, one of two things usually "turn up"—the poorhouse or the jail; for idleness breeds bad habits and clothes a person in rags.

The poor spend-thrift vagabond says to a rich man, "I have discovered there is enough money in the world for all of us, if it was equally divided. This must be done, and we shall all be happy together."

"But," was the response, "if everybody were like you, it would be spent in two months, and what would you do then?"

"Oh! Divide again; keep dividing, of course!" is the reply.

I was recently reading in a London paper an account of a like philosophic pauper who was kicked out of a cheap boarding house, because he could not pay his bill. However, he had a roll of papers sticking out of his coat pocket, which, upon examination, proved to be his plan for paying off the national debt of England—without the aid of a penny. People have got to do as Cromwell said, "Not only trust in Providence, but keep the powder dry." Do your part of the work or you cannot succeed.

Mahomet, one night, while encamping in the desert,

overheard one of his fatigued follower's remark: "I will untie my camel and trust it to God!" "No, no, not so," said the prophet, "*Tie* thy camel and trust it to God!" Do all you can for yourselves, and then trust to Providence or luck, or whatever you please to call it, for the rest.

DEPEND UPON YOUR OWN PERSONAL EXERTIONS

The eye of the employer is often worth more than the hands of a dozen employees. In the nature of things, an agent cannot be so faithful to his employer as to himself. Many who are employers will call to mind instances where the best employees have overlooked important points that could not have escaped their own observation as a proprietor. No person has a right to expect to succeed in life, unless he or she understands his or her business, and no one can understand his or her business thoroughly, unless it is learned by personal application and experience.

A person may be a manufacturer. He or she has got to learn the many details of his or her business personally. They will learn something every day, and they will find that they will make mistakes nearly every day. And these very mistakes are a help in the way of experience, if heeded.

This person will be like the Yankee tin-peddler, who, having been cheated as to quality in the purchase of his merchandise, said, "All right, there's a little information to be gained every day. I will never be cheated in that way again." Thus, this peddler buys his experience and it is the best kind, if not purchased at too dear a rate.

I hold that every person should, like Cuvier, the French naturalist, thoroughly know his or her business. So proficient was he in the study of natural history, that you might bring to him the bone or even a section of a bone of an animal which he had never seen described. He would then, with reasoning from analogy, be able to draw a picture of the object from which the bone had been taken.

On one occasion, his students attempted to deceive him. They rolled one of the students in a cow skin and put him under the professor's table as a new specimen. When the philosopher came into the room, some of the students asked him what animal it was. Suddenly, the animal said, "I am the devil and I am going to eat you." It was but natural that Cuvier should desire to classify this creature, and examining it intently, he said, "Divided hoof; graminivorous! It cannot be done."

He knew that an animal with a split hoof must live upon grass and grain, or other kind of vegetation, and would not be inclined to eat flesh, dead or alive, so he considered himself perfectly safe. The possession of a perfect knowledge of your business is an absolute necessity in order to insure success.

Among the maxims of the elder Rothschild was one, an apparent paradox: "Be cautious and bold." This seems to he a contradiction in terms, but it is not, and there is great wisdom in the maxim. It is, in fact, a condensed statement of what I have already said. It is to say, "You must exercise your caution in laying your plans, but be bold in carrying them out." A person who is all caution will never dare to take hold and be successful; and a person who is all boldness is merely reckless, and must eventually fail. A man or a woman may take a risk and make fifty or one hundred thousand dollars in speculating in stocks, at a single operation. But, if he or she has simple boldness without caution, it is mere chance, and what they gain today, they will lose tomorrow. You must have both the caution and the boldness to insure success.

The Rothschilds have another maxim: "Never have anything to do with an unlucky person or place." That is to say, never have anything to do with a person or place that never succeeds. Because, although a person may appear to be honest and intelligent, if he or she tries this or that thing and always fails, it is on account of some fault or infirmity that you may not be able to discover but, nevertheless, which must exist.

There is no such thing in the world as luck. There never was a person who could go out in the morning and find a purse full of gold in the street today, and another tomorrow, and so on, day after day. This person may do so once in their life; but, as far as mere luck is concerned, they are as liable to lose it as to find it. "Like causes produce like effects." If a man or woman adopts the proper methods to be successful, "luck" will not prevent him or her. If they do not succeed, there are reasons for it, although perhaps, they may not be able to see them.

USE THE BEST TOOLS

When engaging employees, you should be careful to get the best. Understand, you cannot have too good of tools with which to work, and there is no tool you should be so particular about as living tools. If you get a good one, it is better to keep that person than to keep changing. This person learns something every day, and you are benefited by the experience that he or she acquires. This person is worth more to you this year than last, and this person is the last person to part with, provided their habits are good and that they continue faithfully.

However, if, as they get more valuable, they demand

an exorbitant increase of salary on the supposition that you can't do without them, let them go. Whenever I have such an employee, I always discharge them; first, to convince them that their place may be supplied, and second, because they are good for nothing, if they think that they are invaluable and cannot be spared. However, I would keep them, if possible, in order to profit from the result of their experience. An important element in an employee is the brain. You can see signs up, "Help Wanted." However, "help" is not worth a great deal without "heads."

Mr. Henry Ward Beecher illustrates this, in this way:

An employee offers his services by saying, "I have a pair of hands and one of my fingers thinks."

"That is very good," says the employer.

Another man comes along, and says, "I have two fingers that think."

"Ah! That is better."

But a third calls in and says, " I have all my fingers and my thumbs think."

That is better still.

Finally another steps in and says, "I have a brain that thinks; I think all over; I am a thinking *and* working person!"

"You are the person I want," says the delighted employer.

Those employees who have brains and experience are, therefore, the most valuable and not to be readily parted with. It is better for them, as well as yourself, to keep them, at reasonable advances in their salaries from time to time.

DON'T GET ABOVE YOUR BUSINESS

Young people—after they get through their business training or apprenticeship—instead of pursuing their avocation and rising in their business, will often lie about doing nothing.

They say, "I have learned my business, but I am not going to be a hireling. What is the object of learning my trade or profession, unless I establish myself?"

"Have you capital to start with?" I ask.

"No, but I am going to have it," comes the reply.

"How are you going to get it?" I inquire.

"I will tell you confidentially, I have a wealthy old aunt, and she will die pretty soon; but if she does not, I expect to find some rich old man who will lend me a few thousand to give me a start. If I only get the money to start with, I will do well."

There is no greater mistake than when a young man or young woman believes that he or she will succeed with borrowed money. Why? Because every person's experience coincides with that of Mr. Astor's, who said, "It was more difficult for him to accumulate his first thousand dollars, than all the succeeding millions that made up his colossal fortune."

Money is good for nothing, unless you know the value of it by experience. Give a boy twenty thousand dollars and put him in business, and the chances are that he will lose every dollar of it, before he is a year older. Like buying a ticket in the lottery and drawing a prize, it is "easy come, easy go." He does not know the value of it; nothing is worth anything unless it costs effort. Without self-denial and economy, patience and perseverance, and commencing with capital—which you have not earned—you are not sure to succeed in accumulating. Young men and women, instead of waiting for dead men's shoes, you should be up and doing, for there is no class of people who are so unaccommodating in regard to dying as these rich old people, and it is fortunate for the expectant heirs that it is so. Nine out of ten of the rich men of our country today started out in life as poor boys, with determined wills, industry, perseverance, economy, and good habits. They went on gradually, made their own money and saved it; and this is the best way to acquire a fortune.

Stephen Girard started life as a poor cabin boy and died worth nine million dollars. A.T. Stewart was a poor boy who ended up paying taxes on a million and a half dollars of income per year. John Jacob Astor was a poor farmer boy and died worth twenty millions. Cornelius Vanderbilt began life rowing a boat from Staten Island to New York; he presented our government with a steamship worth a million dollars and died worth fifty million.

"There is no royal road to learning," says the proverb, and I may say it is equally true that there is no royal road to wealth. However, I think there is a royal road to both. The road to learning is a royal one; the road that enables the student to expand their intellect and add every day to their stock of knowledge, until, in the pleasant process of intellectual growth, they are able to solve the most profound problems, to count the stars, to analyze every atom of the globe, and to measure the firmament—this is a regal highway, and it is the only road worth traveling.

So, with regard to wealth, go on in confidence; study the rules, and above all things, study human nature; for the proper study of human nature is humans. And you will find that while expanding the intellect and the muscles, your enlarged experience will enable you every day to accumulate more and more principal, which will increase itself by interest and otherwise, until you arrive at a state of independence.

You will find, as a general thing, that the poor boys or girls get rich and the rich boys or girls get poor. For instance, a rich man at his death leaves a large estate to his family. His eldest daughter, who has helped him earn his fortune, knows by experience the value of money, and she takes her inheritance and adds to it. The separate portions of the young children are placed at interest. The little off-springs are patted on the head and told a dozen times a day, "You are rich. You will never have to work, you can always have whatever you wish, for you were born with a golden spoon in your mouth."

The young heirs soon find out what that means; they have the finest dresses and playthings; they are crammed with sugar candies and almost killed with kindness. They pass from school to school, petted and flattered. They become arrogant and self-conceited, abuse their teachers, and carry everything with a high hand. They know noth-ing of the real value of money, having never earned any; but they know all about the "golden spoon" business. At college, they invite their poor fellow students to their room, where they wine and dine them. They are cajoled and caressed and called a glorious good friend, because they are so lavish with their money.

They give fancy dinners, drive fast horses, and invite their friends to parties, determined to have lots of good times. They spend the night in merriment and debauch-ery, and then lead off their companions with the familiar song, "We won't go home till morning." They get their friends to join them in pulling down signs, taking gates from their hinges and throwing them into backyards and horse ponds. If the police arrest them, and take them to jail, they joyfully foot the bill.

"Ah! My friends," they cry, "what is the use of being

rich, if you can't enjoy yourself?"

They might more truly say, "If you can't make a fool of yourself," but they are fast, hate slow things, and don't see the problem.

Young men and women loaded down with other people's money are almost sure to lose all they inherit, and they acquire all sorts of bad habits, which, in the majority of cases, ruin them in health, purse and character. In this country, one generation follows another, and the poor of today are rich in the next generation, or the third. Their experience leads them on, and they become rich, and they leave vast riches to their young children. These children, having been reared in luxury, are inexperienced and get poor; and after long experience, another generation comes on and gathers up riches again in turn. And thus history repeats itself, and happy is the person who, by listening to the experience of others, avoids the rocks and sandbanks on which so many have been wrecked.

LEARN SOMETHING USEFUL

Parents should make their children learn some trade or profession, so that in these days of changing fortunes— of being rich today and poor tomorrow—they may have something tangible to fall back upon. This provision might save many people from misery, who by some unexpected turn of fortune, have lost all their means.

LET HOPE PREDOMINATE, BUT BE NOT TOO VISIONARY

Many people are always kept poor, because they are too visionary. Every project looks to them like certain success, and therefore, they keep changing from one business to another, always in hot water and always "in trouble." The plan of "counting the chickens before they are hatched" is an error of ancient date, but it does not seem to improve by age.

DO NOT SCATTER YOUR POWERS

Engage in one kind of business only, and stick to it faithfully until you succeed, or until your experience shows that you should abandon it. A constant hammering on one nail will generally drive it home at last, so that it can be clinched. When a person's undivided attention is centered on one object, the mind will constantly be suggesting improvements of value, which would escape him or her, if a dozen different subjects occupied his or her brain at once. Many a fortune has slipped through people's fingers, because they were engaged in too many occupations at a time. There is good sense in the old caution against having too many irons in the fire at once.

BE SYSTEMATIC

People should be systematic in their business. A person who does business by rule, having a time and place for everything, doing his or her work promptly, will accomplish twice as much and with half the trouble of one who does it carelessly and slipshod. By introducing system into all your transactions, doing one thing at a time, always meeting appointments with punctuality, you find leisure for pastime and recreation; whereas the one who only half does one thing, and then turns to something else, and half does that, will have his or her business at loose ends, and will never know when the day's work is done—for it never will be done.

Of course, there is a limit to all these rules. We must try to preserve the happy medium, for there is such a thing as being too systematic. There are people, for instance, who put away things so carefully that they can never find them again. It is too much like the "red tape" formality at Washington, and Mr. Dickens' "Circumlocution Office"— all theory and no result.

When the Astor House was first started in New York City, it was undoubtedly the best hotel in the country. The proprietors had learned a good deal in Europe regarding hotels, and the landlords were proud of the rigid system that pervaded every department of their great establishment. When twelve o'clock at night had arrive, and there were a number of guests around, one of the proprietors would say, "Touch that bell, John" and in two minutes, sixty servants with a water bucket in each hand would present themselves in the hall. "This," said the landlord, addressing his guests, "is our fire-bell; it will show you we are quite safe here; we do everything systematically." This was before the Croton water was introduced into the city. But they sometimes carried their system too far. On one occasion, when the hotel was thronged with guests, one of the waiters was suddenly indisposed, and although there were fifty waiters in the hotel, the landlord thought he must have his full complement, or his "system" would be interfered with. Just before dinner time, he rushed downstairs and said, "There must be another waiter. I am one waiter short, what can I do?" He happened to see "Boots," the Irishman. "Pat," said he, "wash your hands and face. Take that white apron and come into the dining-room in five minutes."

Presently, Pat appeared as required, and the proprietor said, "Now Pat, you must stand behind these two chairs, and wait on the gentlemen who will occupy them. Did you ever act as a waiter?"

"I know all about it, sure, but I never did it," replied Pat.

Like the ship's pilot, on one occasion when the captain, thinking he was considerably out of his course asked, "Are you certain you understand what you are doing?" The pilot replied, "Sure and I know every rock in the channel."

That moment, "bang" thumped the vessel against a rock.

"Ah! What do you know, and that is one of 'em, " continued the pilot.

(Nevertheless, let's return to the dining room.) "Pat," said the landlord, "here we do everything systematically. You must first give the gentlemen each a plate of soup, and when they finish that, ask them what they will have next."

Pat replied in his Irish brogue, "Ah! An' I understand parfectly the vartues of a shystem."

Very soon, in came the guests. The plates of soup were placed before them. One of Pat's two gentlemen ate his soup; the other did not care for it. He said, "Waiter, take this plate away and bring me some fish." Pat looked at the untasted plate of soup, and remembering the injunctions of the landlord in regard to "system," replied, "Not till ye have ate yer supe!"

Of course, that was carrying "the system" entirely too far.

READ THE NEWSPAPERS

Always take a trustworthy newspaper, and thus keep thoroughly posted with regard to the transactions of the world. The person who is without a newspaper is cut off from their species. In these days of telegraphs and steam, many important inventions and improvements in every branch of trade are being made, and those who don't consult the newspapers will soon find themselves—and their business—left out in the cold.

BEWARE OF "OUTSIDE OPERATIONS"

We sometimes see people who have obtained fortunes suddenly become poor. In many cases, this arises from intemperance, and often from gaming, and other bad habits. Frequently, it occurs because people have been engaged in outside operations, of some sort. When they get rich in their legitimate business, they are told of a grand speculation where they can make a score of thousands. Their friends, who tell them that they are born lucky and that everything they touch turns into gold, constantly flatter them. Now, if they forget that their economical habits, moral strength of conduct, and personal attention to business that caused their success in life, they will listen to the siren voices.

They say, "We'll put in twenty thousand dollars. We have been lucky, and good luck will soon bring us back sixty thousand dollars." A few days elapse and it is discovered they must put in ten thousand dollars more; soon after they are told "it is all right," but certain matters not foreseen require an advance of twenty thousand dollars more, which will bring them a rich harvest. However, before the time comes around to realize, the bubble bursts, they lose all they are possessed of, and then they learn what they ought to have known at the first. That is that however successful people may be in their own business, if they turn from that and engage in a business which they don't understand, they are like Samson when shorn of his locks, his strength departed and he becomes like any other person.

A person who has plenty of money ought to invest something in everything that appears to promise success and that will probably benefit humankind. However, let the sums invested be moderate in amount, and never let a person foolishly jeopardize a fortune that has been earned in a legitimate way, by investing in things in which he or she has had no experience.

DON'T ENDORSE WITHOUT SECURITY

I hold that no person ought ever to endorse a note or become security for anyone, be it his father, brother, mother or sister, to a greater extent than he or she can afford to lose and care nothing about, without taking good security.

Here is a man that is worth twenty thousand dollars; he is doing a thriving manufacturing or mercantile trade. You are retired and living on your money. This man comes to you and says, "You are aware that I am worth twenty thousand dollars, and don't owe a dollar. If I had five thousand dollars in cash, I could purchase a particular lot of goods and double my money in a couple of months. Will you endorse my note for that amount?"

You reflect that he is worth twenty thousand dollars, and you incur no risk by endorsing his note. You would like to accommodate him, and you lend your name—without taking the precaution of getting security. Shortly after, he shows you the note with your endorsement canceled, and tells you, probably truly, that he made the profit that he expected by the operation. You reflect that you have done a good action, and the thought makes you feel happy. By and by, the same thing occurs again and you do it again. You have already fixed the impression in your mind that it is perfectly safe to endorse his notes without security.

But the trouble is this man is getting money too easily. He has only to take your note to the bank, get it discounted and take the cash. He gets money for the time being without effort—without inconvenience to himself. Now, mark the result. He sees a chance for speculation, outside of his business. A temporary investment of only $10,000 is required. It is sure to come back, before a note at the bank would be due. He places a note for that amount before you. You sign it almost mechanically. Being firmly convinced that your friend is responsible and trustworthy, you endorse his notes as a matter of course.

Unfortunately, the speculation does not come to a head quite so soon as was expected, and another $10,000 note must be discounted to take up the last one when due. Before this note matures, the speculation has proved an utter failure and all the money is lost. Does the loser tell his friend, the endorser, that he has lost half of his fortune? Not at all. He doesn't even mention that he has speculated at all. But, he has gotten excited; the spirit of speculation has seized him; he sees others making large sums in this way (we seldom hear of the losers), and, like other speculators, he looks for his money where he loses it. He tries again. Endorsing notes has become chronic with you, and at every loss, he gets your signature for whatever amount he wants. Finally, you discover your friend has lost all of his property and all of yours. You are overwhelmed with astonishment and grief, and you say, "It is a hard thing; my friend here has ruined me." But, you should add, "I have also ruined him." If you had said in the first place, "I will accommodate you, but I never endorse without taking ample security," he could not have gone beyond the length of his tether, and he would never have been tempted away from his legitimate business. It is a very dangerous thing, therefore, at any time, to let people get possession of money too easily. It tempts them to hazardous speculations, if nothing more.

So, with the person starting in business, let him or her understand the value of money by earning it. When that person understands its value, then grease the wheels a little in helping to start the business, but remember, people who get money too easily, cannot usually succeed. You must get the first dollars by hard knocks, and at some sacrifice, in order to appreciate the value of those dollars.

ADVERTISE YOUR BUSINESS

We all depend, more or less, upon the public for our support. We all trade with the public—lawyers, doctors, shoemakers, artists, blacksmiths, showmen, opera singers, railroad presidents, and college professors. Those who deal with the public must be careful that their goods are valuable, that they are genuine, and will give satisfaction.

When you get an article that you know is going to please your customers and that, when they have tried it, they will feel they have gotten their money's worth, then let the fact be known that you have got it! Be careful to advertise it in some shape or other, because it is evident that if a person has ever so good an article for sale, and nobody knows it, it will bring to him or her no return. In a country like this, where nearly everybody reads, and where newspapers are issued and circulated in editions of five thousand to two hundred thousand, it would be very unwise if this channel were not taken advantage of to reach the public in advertising.

A newspaper goes into the family and is read by wife and children, as well as the head of the home; hence hundreds and thousands of people may read your advertisement, while you are attending to your routine business. Many, perhaps, read it while you are asleep. The whole philosophy of life is: First sow, then reap. That is the way the farmer does. He plants his potatoes and corn, sows his grain, and then goes about something else, and the time comes when he reaps. But, he never reaps first and sows afterwards.

This principle applies to all kinds of business and to nothing more eminently than to advertising. If a person has a genuine article, there is no way in which he or she can reap more advantageously than by "sowing" to the public in this way. It must, of course, be a really good article, and one that will please the customers. Anything spurious will not succeed permanently, because the public is wiser than many imagine. Men and women are selfish, and we all prefer purchasing where we can get the most for our money, and we try to find out where we can most surely do so.

You may advertise a spurious article and induce many people to call and buy it once, but they will denounce you as an imposter and swindler, and your business will gradually die out and leave you poor. This is right. Few people can safely depend upon chance custom. You all need to have your customers return and purchase again.

A man said to me, "I have tried advertising and did not succeed; yet, I have a good article."

I replied, "My friend, there may be exceptions to a general rule. But how do you advertise?"

"I put it in a weekly newspaper three times, and paid a dollar and a half for it," said the man.

I replied, "Sir, advertising is like learning: A little is a dangerous thing!"

A French writer says that, "The reader of a newspaper does not see the first mention of an ordinary advertisement. The second insertion the reader sees, but does not read. The third insertion, the reader reads and the fourth insertion, the reader looks at the price. The fifth insertion, the reader speaks of it to his or her spouse. The sixth insertion, the reader is ready to purchase, and the seventh insertion, the reader purchases."

Your object in advertising is to make the public understand what you have got to sell, and if you have not the pluck to keep advertising, until you have imparted that information, all the money you have spent is lost. You are like the fellow who told the gentleman if he would give him ten cents, it would save him a dollar.

"How can I help you so much with so small a sum?" asked the gentleman in surprise.

"I started out this morning (hiccuped the fellow) with the full determination to get drunk, and I have spent my only dollar to accomplish the object, and it has not quite done it. Ten cents worth more of whiskey would just do it, and in this manner, I should save the dollar already expended."

Therefore, a person who advertises at all must keep it up, until the public knows who this person is, what he or she is selling, and what the business is, or else the money invested in advertising is lost. Some people have a peculiar genius for writing a striking advertisement, one that will arrest the attention of the reader at first sight. This fact, of course, gives the advertiser a great advantage.

Sometimes a person makes himself popular by a unique sign or a curious display in his window.

Recently, I observed a swing sign extending over the sidewalk in front of a store, on which was the inscription in plain letters,

"DON'T READ THE OTHER SIDE"

Of course, I did and so did everybody else. And I learned that this person became successful by first attracting the public to his business in that way, and then using his customers well afterwards.

Genin, the hatter, bought the first Jenny Lind ticket at auction for two hundred and twenty-five dollars, because he knew it would be a good advertisement for him. "Who is the bidder?" said the auctioneer, as he knocked down that ticket at Castle Garden. "Genin, the hatter," was the response. Here were thousands of people from Fifth Avenue and from distant cities in the highest stations in life. "Who is Genin, the hatter?" they exclaimed. They had never heard of him before. The next morning the newspapers and telegraph had circulated the facts from Maine to Texas. From five to ten million people read that the tickets sold at auction for Jenny Lind's first concert amounted to about twenty thousand dollars, and that a single ticket was sold at two hundred and twenty-five dollars to Genin, the hatter.

Men throughout the country involuntarily took off their hats to see if they had a Genin hat on their heads. At a town in Iowa, it was found that in the crowd around the post office, there was one man who had a Genin hat, and he showed it in triumph, although it was worn out and not worth two cents. "Why," one man exclaimed, "you have a real Genin hat. What a lucky fellow you are." Another man said, "Hang on to that hat, it will be a valuable heirloom in your family."

Still another man in the crowd, who seemed to envy the possessor of this good fortune, said, "Come, give us all a chance; put it up at auction!" He did so, and it was sold as a keepsake for nine dollars and fifty cents! What was the consequence to Mr. Genin? He sold ten thousand extra hats per annum the first six years. Nine-tenths of the purchasers bought of him, probably out of curiosity, and many of them, finding that he gave them an equivalent for their money, became his regular customers. This novel advertisement first struck their attention, and then, as he made a good article, they came again.

Now, I don't say that everybody should advertise as Mr. Genin did. But, I do say that if people have goods for sale, and they don't advertise them in some way, the chances are that some day the sheriff will do it for them. Nor do I say that everybody must advertise in a newspaper or indeed use "printer's ink" at all. On the contrary, although that article is indispensable in the majority of cases, doctors, clergymen, lawyers and some others can more effectually reach the public in some other manner. However, it is obvious they must be known in some way, else how could they be supported?

BE POLITE AND KIND
TO YOUR CUSTOMERS

Politeness and civility are the best capital ever invested in business. Large stores, gilt signs, and flaming advertisements will all prove unavailing, if you or your employees treat your patrons abruptly. The truth is, the more kind and liberal a person is, the more generous will be the patronage bestowed upon them.

Like begets like. The person who gives the greatest amount of goods of a corresponding quality for the least sum (still reserving for him or herself a profit) will generally succeed best in the long run. This brings us to the golden rule, "As ye would that men should do to you, do ye also to them." They will do better by you than if you always treated them as if you wanted to get the most you could out of them for the least return.

People who drive sharp bargains with their customers, acting as if they never expected to see them again, will not be mistaken. They will never see them again as customers. People don't like to pay and get kicked also.

One of the ushers in my Museum once told me he intended to whip a man who was in the lecture room, as soon as he came out. I inquired, "What for?"

"Because he said I was no gentleman," replied the usher.

"Never mind," I replied, "he pays for that, and you will not convince him you are a gentleman by whipping him. I cannot afford to lose a customer. If you whip him, he will never visit the Museum again, and he will induce friends to go with him to other places of amusement instead of this, and thus you see, I should be a serious loser."

"But he insulted me," muttered the usher.

"Exactly," I replied, "and if he owned the Museum and you had paid him for the privilege of visiting it, and he had then insulted you, there might be some reason in your resenting it. However, in this instance, he is the man who pays, while we receive, and you must, therefore, put up with his bad manners."

My usher laughingly remarked that this was undoubtedly the true policy, but he added that he should not object to an increase of salary, if he were expected to be abused, in order to promote my interest.

BE CHARITABLE

Of course, people should be charitable, because it is a duty and a pleasure. But, even as a matter of policy, if you possess no higher incentive, you will find that the liberal person will command patronage, while the sordid, uncharitable miser will be avoided. Solomon says, "There is that scattereth and yet increaseth; and there is that withholdeth more than meet, but it tendeth to poverty." Of course, the only true charity is that which is from the heart.

The best kind of charity is to help those who are willing to help themselves. Promiscuous almsgiving, without inquiring into the worthiness of the applicant, is bad in every sense. But to search out and quietly assist those who are struggling for themselves is the kind that "scattereth and yet increaseth." But don't fall into the idea that some people practice of giving a prayer instead of a potato and a benediction instead of bread to the hungry. It is easier to make Christians with full stomachs than empty.

DON'T BLAB

Some people have a foolish habit of telling their business secrets. If they make money, they like to tell their neighbors how it was done. Nothing is gained by this and, oftentimes, much is lost. Say nothing about your profits, your hopes, your expectations, or your intentions. This should also apply to letters, as well as to conversation.

Goethe makes Mephistophiles say, "Never write a letter nor destroy one." Business people must write letters, but they should be careful what they put in them. If you are losing money, be especially cautious and not tell of it, or you will lose your reputation.

PRESERVE YOUR INTEGRITY

It is more precious than diamonds or rubies. The old miser said to his sons: "Get money; get it honestly, if you can, but get money." This advice was not only atrociously wicked, but it was the very essence of stupidity. It was as much as to say, "If you find it difficult to obtain money honestly, you can easily get it dishonestly. Get it in that way." Poor fool!

He is a poor fool not to know that the most difficult thing in life is to make money dishonestly. He is a poor fool not to know that our prisons are full of men and women who attempted to follow this advice. He is a poor fool not to understand that no man or woman can be dishonest, without soon being found out, and that when their lack of principle is discovered, nearly every avenue to success is closed against them forever.

The public very properly shuns all whose integrity is doubted. No matter how polite, pleasant and accommodating a person may be, none of us dare to deal with him or her, if we suspect "false weights and measures." Strict honesty not only lies at the foundation of all success in life (financially), but in every other respect.

Uncompromising integrity of character is invaluable. It secures to its possessor a peace and joy which cannot be attained without it—which no amount of money or houses and lands can purchase. A person, who is known to be strictly honest, may be ever so poor, but he or she has the purses of all the community at his or her disposal. All know that if they promise to return what they borrow, they will never disappoint them.

As a mere matter of selfishness, therefore, if a person had no higher motive for being honest, all will find that the maxim of Dr. Franklin can never fail to be true, that "honesty is the best policy." To get rich is not always equivalent to being successful. There are many "rich-poor" men and woman. And there are many others, honest and devout, who have never possessed so much money as some rich people squander in a week. Yet, they are nevertheless really richer and happier than any person can ever be, who is an offender of the higher laws of their being.

The inordinate love of money, no doubt, may be and is the root of all evil. However, money itself, when properly used, is not only a handy thing to have in the house, but also affords the gratification of blessing our race by enabling its possessor to enlarge the scope of human happiness and human influence. The desire for wealth is nearly universal, and none can say it is not commendable, provided the possessor of it accepts its responsibilities, and uses it as a friend to humanity.

The history of money-getting, which is commerce, is a history of civilization, and wherever trade has flourished most, there, too, have art and science produced the noblest fruits. In fact, as a general thing, money-getters are the benefactors of our race. To them, in a great measure, are we indebted for our institutions of learning and of art, our academies, colleges, and churches. It is no argument against the desire for or the possession of wealth to say that there are sometimes misers who hoard money, only for the sake of hoarding, and who have no higher aspiration than to grasp everything that comes within their reach. As we have sometimes hypocrites in religion and demagogues in politics, so there are occasionally misers among money-getters. These, however, are only exceptions to the general rule.

However, when in this country, we find such a nuisance and stumbling block as a miser, we remember with gratitude that in America, we have no laws of heritage. And in the due course of nature, the time will come when the hoarded dust will be scattered for the benefit of humankind.

To all people, therefore, do I conscientiously say— make money honestly and not otherwise, for Shakespeare has truly said, "He who wants money, means, and content is without three good friends."

RUSSELL CONWELL
A BIOGRAPHY

ebruary 15, 1843 was a cold and wintry day in the
Eastern Berkshires of Massachusetts. But in one small
house, it was a little warmer and brighter. That was the
day that Russell Conwell entered this world.

Conwell grew up to be a soldier, a lawyer, a lecturer, an
editor, a philanthropist, the founder of Temple University,
and the author of one of the most memorable speeches,
Acres of Diamonds.

As a young boy, his family's house was a station on the
Underground Railway. Here, he watched slaves make their
way to freedom with the help of his father. Conwell met
Frederick Douglas, the abolitionist and orator, and later
became friends with John Brown. As a soldier, he met
Abraham Lincoln and was present at the great President's
funeral.

Watching people sacrifice their lives for others and
their own beliefs; witnessing the actions of Johnnie Ring—
the legendary Civil War soldier who lost his life while trying to protect Conwell's sword during a heated battle
between the North and South—made an impact on
Conwell. He said, "It was through Johnnie Ring and his

giving his life through devotion to me that I became a Christian. This did not come about immediately, but it came before the war was over, and it came through faithful Johnnie Ring." It was also at that time that he dedicated himself to achieving success in his own life and helping others do the same.

After the war, Conwell experienced numerous accomplishments, as well as failures. His "up and down" lifestyle continued for many years, until he became an attorney and built up a steady, lucrative practice. Yet, he felt unfulfilled. He had helped himself to become a success, but what had he done for anyone else? Ultimately, the answer came to him. At the age of forty, he made a decision that would change his life and the lives of hundreds of thousands of people all over the country.

Conwell abandoned his profitable legal practice to become the minister of a small church. He agreed to become the preacher of this congregation for the small sum of $600. Wanting to help, but also very much aware of the need to put food on the table (and ever the wise businessperson), Conwell had the church agree to double his salary, whenever he doubled the church membership. His ability to speak and move people with his words was just what this struggling church needed.

Double the membership he did. And then, it doubled again. The more the church grew, the larger the salary Conwell received. It actually got to be embarrassing for the church deacons that they were paying him so much, but Conwell was living up to his side of the "deal," and so did they.

It was at this time that another struggling church came along, with the potential for a very large membership. They offered Conwell the same arrangement that he had with his current church and when he accepted the pastorship with them, the same result occurred. Eventually, this previously struggling church also grew to having an overflowing congregation. The pews filled twice every Sunday with churchgoers, as well as those who were just plain curious to hear what Conwell had to say.

Conwell's preaching style was not the "heavy theory" and "theological mish-mash" that other preachers would use to try to impress their congregations. Instead, Conwell preached in an easy to understand language and embellished his sermons with humor and stories. He didn't stand bchind a pulpit. He went out to the people and let them hear the message of the Gospels in a simple, yet powerful and energetic way. When Conwell spoke, people listened.

Conwell once said about his preaching, "Always remember, as you preach, that you are striving to save at least one soul with every sermon. I feel, whenever I preach, that there is always one person in the congregation to whom, in all probability, I shall never preach again, and therefore I feel that I must exert my utmost power in that last chance."

With the congregation still growing and more services being added, Conwell's fee was, due to his arrangement, skyrocketing. The deacons were happy with the former and concerned about the later. Therefore, the deacons asked Conwell if they could amend their previous contract. The new terms would state that Conwell would preach whenever he could, but he would also be allowed to take outside speaking engagements whenever he wished. In turn, the church would pay him $10,000 dollars a year for life.

Conwell, knowing a good deal when he saw it, agreed

to the amendment. He would be freed from the routine pressures and commitments of a regular pastorship, and could now deliver his message of hope and success on a broader scope to others who desperately needed to hear it.

That message of hope and success was delivered to the masses in the form of Conwell's phenomenal speech, *Acres of Diamonds*. In *Acres of Diamonds*, Conwell attacked some of the myths regarding wealth and success that many believed in then—and still do today. For example, in order to start or grow a business, many people felt that they had to move from where they were born and raised to a larger, more populous city or that if they only had a large amount of capital, they would be more successful.

Having met many successful people during his travels, Conwell knew that those beliefs were unfounded. He had personally known many wealthy business people who had started flourishing businesses in their own hometown—and with very little money. Said Conwell, "To be great, you must begin where you are and with what you are . . . right now!"

Conwell attacked these myths and other popular misconceptions, such as the old adage that people who inherit money will always remain rich and those that don't inherit money will always remain poor. To this, Conwell would shout, "There is no class of people to be pitied so much as the inexperienced sons and daughters of the rich of our generation." Many people who inherit money squander it and lose it, while others who have worked hard for it keep it and use it for the betterment of society.

Personally, I admire Conwell's "straight-from-the-hip", "take no prisoners" style of delivery. He spoke what he believed with zest and power. And people listened . . . and learned that he was right!

Wherever he went, Conwell was a big hit. He was one of the most requested speakers on the Chautauqua and Lyceum circuit—which would evolve into the lecture and speakers' circuit that we have today. Unlike other famous speakers who would only lecture in big towns and cities, Conwell would also travel to small towns, churches, and villages. He took his message to wherever the people were willing to listen. Whenever and wherever Conwell would speak, people would come from miles around to hear his voice and his message. And the halls where he spoke were always filled beyond capacity.

Even with this popularity, Conwell never got the huge publicity of other speakers, primarily because the media felt that he spoke to "common folk." Conwell could have cared less. He preferred to deliver his message to those who needed to hear it. His "magnificent obsession" was to bring his message to as many people as he could.

The fees that he received were quite impressive, but having already made more money than he would ever need, Conwell would subtract his expenses from his fees and then give the rest of the money to some young man who couldn't afford a college education. (Not many women attended college at that time.)

"Every night," Conwell said, "when my lecture is over and the check is in my hand, I sit down in my room in the hotel. I then subtract from the total sum received my actual expenses for that place, and make out a check for the difference and send it to some young man on my list. And, I always send with the check a letter of advice and helpfulness, expressing my hope that it will be of some service to him and telling him that he is to feel under no obligation, except to his Lord. I feel strongly, and I try to make every young man feel, that there must be no sense of obligation to me, personally. And I tell them that I am hoping to leave behind me men who will do more work than I have done. Don't think that I put in too much advice," Conwell added, "for I only try to let them know that a friend is trying to help them."

While taking a respite in Philadelphia, Conwell was approached by a few young people who expressed an interest in having him teach them his business and success secrets, on a private basis. Conwell agreed. As word of his private teachings spread, more students yearned to be taught. As his private classes began to grow, Conwell found that many of his students were also interested in a variety of other subjects. When Conwell began to include other instructors and more subjects, the student body of this informal learning establishment quickly began to expand.

To handle the demand, more teachers were added—which brought more students. It wasn't long before a few buildings were constructed and connected to his church. These buildings formed the beginning of Temple University—a university, which, at that time, dedicated itself to giving an education to those who were unable to get it through the usual channels.

Conwell was an amazing man. He worked 16-hour days, up until his passing at the age of 82. Conwell always thought big. He dreamed big, thought big, and won big. He never understood why so many people never tried to achieve great things. Conwell would say, "The same effort that wins a small success would, rightly directed, have won a great success. Think big things and then do them!"

Yet, he also knew that success took time. One of his favorite sayings was, "Let Patience have her perfect work." He would say it over and over again, not only to remind others that they needed to be patient, but to also remind himself that *he* needed to be patient, when things didn't happen as soon as he would have liked.

With his passing in 1925, Conwell left a legacy. Today, Temple University is a major educational institution, known and respected throughout the world. His wonderful speech, *Acres of Diamonds,* lives on as a tribute to the man who made his own wealth, success, and happiness—by trying to help others do the same. Even though this edition of his speech was from a presentation that he gave in his beloved Philadelphia, the message applies to every city, town, and village in America today.

On September 1, 1913, in South Worthington, Mass., Russell Conwell wrote: "The hand which now holds this pen must in the natural course of events soon cease to gesture on the platform, and it is a sincere, prayerful hope that this book will go on into the years doing increasing good for the aid of my brothers and sisters in the human family."

It is with this thought in mind that I hope that you enjoy and learn from this edition of *Acres of Diamonds*.

I express gratitude for the inclusion of information from the book, "His Life and Achievements" by Robert Shackleton, 1915 and "We Called it Culture—The Story of Chautauqua" by Victoria Case and Robert Ormond Case (Publishers: Doubleday & Company, New York, 1948), as well as other documents and sources. To hear an audio recording of Russell H. Conwell delivering a portion of his *Acres of Diamonds* speech, visit http://historymatters.gmu.edu/d/5768/ on the Internet, courtesy of the Michigan State University Voice Library.

ACRES OF DIAMONDS

BY RUSSELL H. CONWELL

ACRES OF DIAMONDS

In 1870, we went down the Tigris and Euphrates rivers. Along with a party of English travelers, I found myself under the direction of an old guide whom we hired up at Baghdad. I have often thought how that guide resembled our barbers in certain mental characteristics. He thought that it was not only his duty to guide us down those rivers and do what he was paid for doing, but also to entertain us with stories curious and weird, ancient and modern, strange and familiar. Many of them I have forgotten, and I am glad I have, but there is one I shall never forget.

The old guide was leading my camel by its halter along the banks of those ancient rivers, and he told me story after story until I grew weary of his story-telling and ceased to listen. (I had never been irritated with that guide when he lost his temper, as I ceased listening.) Nevertheless, I remember that he took off his Turkish cap and swung it in a circle to get my attention. I could see it through the corner of my eye, but I determined not to look straight at him for fear he would tell another story. I did finally look, and as soon as I did, he went right into another story. Said he, "I will tell you a story now which I reserve for my particular friends." When he emphasized the words "particular friends," I listened, and I have ever been glad I did. I really feel devoutly thankful that there are 1,674 young men who have been carried through college by this lecture, who are also glad that I did listen.

The old guide told me that there once lived, not far from the River Indus, an ancient man by the name of Ali Hafed. He said that Ali Hafed owned a very large farm; that he had orchards, grain fields, and gardens; that he had money at interest, and was a wealthy and contented man. He was contented because he was wealthy and wealthy because he was contented. One day there visited that old Persian farmer, one of these ancient Buddhist priests, one of the wise men of the East. He sat down by the fire and told the old farmer how the world of ours was made.

He said that this world was once a mere bank of fog, and that the Almighty thrust His finger into this bank of fog, and began slowly to move His finger around, increasing the speed until at last He whirled this bank of fog into a solid ball of fire. Then it went rolling through the universe, burning its way through other banks of fog, and condensed the moisture without, until it fell in floods of rain upon its hot surface, and cooled the outward crust. Then the internal fires bursting outward through the crust threw up the mountains and hills, the valleys, the plains and prairies of this wonderful world of ours. If this internal molten mass came bursting out and cooled very quickly it became granite; less quickly copper, less quickly silver, less quickly gold, and, after gold, diamonds were made. Said the old priest, "A diamond is a congealed drop of sunlight."

This is a scientific truth; a diamond is an actual deposit of carbon from the sun. The old priest told Ali Hafed that if he had one diamond the size of his thumb, he could purchase the county, and if he had a mine of diamonds, he could place his children upon thrones through the influence of their great wealth.

Ali Hafed heard all about diamonds, how much they were worth, and went to his bed that night a poor man. He had not lost anything, but he was poor because he was discontented, and discontented because he feared he was poor. He said, "I want a mine of diamonds," and he lay awake all night. Early in the morning, he sought out the priest.

Now, I know by experience that a priest is very cross when awakened early in the morning, and when he shook that old priest out of his dreams, Ali Hafed said to him, "Will you tell me where I can find diamonds?"

"Diamonds!" shouted the priest, "What do you want with diamonds?"

"Why, I wish to be immensely rich," said Al Hafed, "but I don't know where to find them."

The priest said, "Well, if you will find a river that runs through white sands, between high mountains, in those white sands you will always find diamonds."

"I don't believe there is any such river," said Ali Hafed.

The priest responded, "Oh yes, there are plenty of them. All you have to do is to go and find them, and then you have them."

Said Ali Hafed, "I will go."

So Hafed sold his farm, collected his money, left his family in charge of a neighbor, and away he went in search of diamonds. He began his search, very properly to my mind, at the Mountains of the Moon. Afterward, Hafed came around into Palestine, then wandered on into Europe, and at last when his money was all spent and he was in rags, wretchedness, and poverty, Hafed stood on the shore of that bay at Barcelona, in Spain. Suddenly a great tidal wave came rolling in between the pillars of Hercules, and the poor, afflicted, suffering, dying Hafed could not resist the awful temptation to cast himself into that incoming tide. He did, and Ali Hafed sank beneath its foaming crest, never to rise in this life again.

When that old guide had finished that awfully sad story, he stopped the camel I was riding on and went back to fix the baggage that was coming off another camel. I had an opportunity to muse over his story while he was gone. I remember saying to myself, "Why did he reserve that story for his 'particular friends'?" There seemed to be no beginning, no middle, no end, nothing to it. That was the first story I had ever heard told in my life, and it would be the first one I ever read, in which the hero was killed in the first chapter. I had but one chapter of that story, and the hero was dead.

When the guide came back and took up the halter of my camel, he went right ahead with the story, into the second chapter, just as though there had been no break. The man who purchased Ali Hafed's farm one day led his camel into the garden to drink, and as that camel put its nose into the shallow water of that garden brook, Ali Hafed's successor noticed a curious flash of light from the white sands of the stream. He pulled out a black stone having an eye of light reflecting all the hues of the rainbow. He took the pebble into the house and put it on the mantel which covers the central fires, and forgot all about it.

A few days later, this same old priest came in to visit Ali Hafed's successor, and the moment he opened that drawing room door, he saw that flash of light on the mantel. The priest rushed up to it and shouted: "Here is a diamond! Has Ali Hafed returned?"

"Oh no," said Hafed's successor, "Ali Hafed has not returned, and that is not a diamond. That is nothing but a stone we found right out here in our own garden."

"But," said the priest, "I tell you, I know a diamond when I see it. I know positively that is a diamond."

Then together they rushed out into that old garden and stirred up the white sands with their fingers, and lo! There came up other gems—more beautiful and valuable than the first. "Thus," said the guide to me—and, friends, it is historically true—"was discovered the diamond mine of Golconda, the most magnificent diamond mine in all the history of mankind, excelling the Kimberly itself. The Kohinoor and the Orloff of the crown jewels of England and Russia, the largest on earth, came from that mine."

When that old guide told me the second chapter of his story, he then took off his cap and swung it around in the air again to get my attention to the moral.

As he swung his hat, he said to me, "Had Ali Hafed remained at home and dug in his own cellar, or underneath his own wheat fields, or in his own garden, instead of wretchedness, starvation, and death by suicide in a strange land, he would have had 'acres of diamonds.' For every acre of that old farm, yes every shovel full, afterward revealed gems which since have decorated the crowns of monarchs."

When he had added the moral to his story, I saw why he reserved it for his "particular friends." However, I did not tell him I could see it. It was his way of going around a thing like a lawyer, to say indirectly what he did not dare say directly, that "in his private opinion" there was a certain young man then traveling down the Tigris River that might better be at home in America.

I did not tell him I could see that, but I told him his story reminded me of one, and I told it to him quick, and I think I will tell it to you.

I told him of a man out in California in 1847 who owned a ranch. He heard they had discovered gold in southern California, and so with a passion for gold he sold his ranch to Colonel Sutter, and away he went, never to come back.

Colonel Sutter put a mill upon a stream that ran through that ranch, and one day his little girl brought some wet sand from the raceway into their home and sifted it through her fingers before the fire, and in that falling sand a visitor saw the first shining scales of real gold that were ever discovered in California. The man who had owned that ranch wanted gold, and he could have secured it for the mere taking. Indeed, thirty-eight millions of dollars has been taken out of a very few acres since then.

About eight years ago, I delivered this lecture in a city that stands on that farm, and they told me that a one-third owner for years and years had been getting one hundred and twenty dollars in gold every fifteen minutes, sleeping or waking, without taxation. You and I would enjoy an income like that!

But, the best illustration that I have now of this thought was found here in our own Pennsylvania. There was a man living in Pennsylvania, not unlike some Pennsylvanians you have seen, who owned a farm, and he did with that farm just what I should do with a farm, if I owned one in Pennsylvania—he sold it. However, before he sold it he decided to secure employment collecting coal oil for his cousin who was in the business in Canada, where they first discovered oil on this continent. They dipped it from the running streams at that early time. So, this Pennsylvania farmer wrote to his cousin asking for employment. You see, friends, this farmer was not altogether a foolish man. No, he was not. He did not leave his farm, until he had something else to do.

Of all the simpletons the stars shine on, I don't know of a worse one than the person who leaves one job before he or she has another. When he wrote to his cousin for employment, his cousin replied, "I cannot engage you, because you know nothing about the oil business."

Well, then the old farmer said, "I will know," and with most commendable zeal, he set himself at the study of the whole subject. He began away back at the second day of God's creation when this world was covered thick and deep with that primitive vegetation to the coal oil stage, until he knew all he could about it. "Now," said he in his letter to his cousin, "I understand the oil business." His cousin answered, "All right, come on."

Therefore, he sold his farm, according to the county record, for $833 (even money, no cents). He had scarcely gone from that place before the man who purchased the spot went out to arrange for the watering of the cattle. He found the previous owner had gone out years before and put a plank across the brook back of the barn, edgewise into the surface of the water just a few inches. The purpose of that plank at that sharp angle across the brook was to throw over to the other bank a dreadful looking scum through which the cattle would not put their noses. But with that plank there to throw it all over to one side, the cattle would drink below.

Thus that man who had gone to Canada had been himself damming back for twenty-three years a flood of coal oil which the state geologists of Pennsylvania declared to us—ten years later—was even then worth a hundred million dollars to our state, and four years ago our geologist declared the discovery to be worth to our state a thousand million dollars. The man who owned that territory on which the city of Titusville now stands, and those Pleasantville valleys, had studied the subject from the second day of God's creation clear down to the present time. He studied it until he knew all about it, and yet he is said to have sold the whole of it for $833, and again I say, "no sense."

But I need another illustration, and I found it in Massachusetts, and I am sorry I did because that is my old state. This young man in Massachusetts furnishes another phase of my thought. He went to Yale College and studied mines and mining, and became so adept as a mining engineer that he was employed by the authorities of the university to train students who were behind in their classes. During his senior year, he earned $15 a week for doing that work. When he graduated, they raised his pay from $15 to $45 a week, and offered him a professorship.

He ran straight home to his mother and said, "Mother, I won't work for $45 a week. The idea of a man with a brain like mine working for $45 a week. Let's go out to California and stake out gold mines and silver mines and be immensely rich."

Said his mother, "Now, Charlie, it is just as well to be happy as it is to be rich."

"Yes," said Charlie, "but it is just as well to be rich and happy, too." And they were both right about it.

As he was an only son and she a widow, of course he had his way. They always do. They sold out in Massachusetts and instead of going to California, they went to Wisconsin, where he went into the employ of the Superior Copper Mining Company at $15 a week again, but with the provision in his contract that he should have an interest in any mines he should discover for the company. I don't believe he ever discovered a mine, and if I am looking in the face of any stockholder of that copper company, you wish he had discovered something or other. I have friends who are not here because they could not afford a ticket, who did have stock in that company at the time this young man was employed there. This young man went out there, and I have not heard a word from him. I don't know what became of him, and I don't know whether he found any mines or not, but I don't believe he ever did. However, I do know the other end of the line. He had scarcely gotten out of the old homestead before the succeeding owner went out to dig potatoes. The potatoes were already growing in the ground when he bought the farm, and as the old farmer was bringing in a basket of potatoes, it hugged very tight between the ends of the stone fence.

You know in Massachusetts our farms are nearly all stone walls. There you are obliged to be very economical of front gateways, in order to have some place to put the stone. When that basket hugged so tight, he set it down on the ground, and then dragged on one side and pulled on the other side, and as he was dragging that basket through, this farmer noticed in the upper and outer corner of that stone wall, right next the gate, a block of native silver eight inches square. That professor of mines, mining, and mineralogy who knew so much about the subject that he would not work for $45 a week, when he sold that homestead in Massachusetts, sat right on that silver to make the bargain. He was born on that homestead, was brought up there, and had gone back and forth rubbing the stone with his sleeve until it reflected his countenance, and seemed to say, "Here is a hundred thousand dollars right down here just for the taking." But he would not take it. The silver was right there in his home in Newburyport, Massachusetts, not all away off in California or anywhere else. And he was a professor of mineralogy!

My friends, that mistake is very universally made, and why should we even smile at him. I often wonder what has become of him. I do not know at all, but I will tell you what I "guess," as a Yankee. I guess that he sits out there by his fireside tonight with his friends gathered around him, and he is saying to them something like this: "Do you know that man Conwell who lives in Philadelphia?"

"Oh yes, I have heard of him," say his friends.

"Do you know that man Jones that lives in Philadelphia?" asks the man.

To which his friends reply, "Yes, we have heard of him, too."

Then the man begins to laugh, shakes his head from side to side, and says to his friends, "Well, they have done just the same thing I did, precisely." And that spoils the whole joke, for you and I have done the same thing he did, and while we sit here and laugh at him, he has a better right to sit out there and laugh at us. I know I have made the same mistakes, but of course, that does not make any difference, because we don't expect the same man to preach and practice, too.

As I come here tonight and look around this audience, I am seeing again what through these fifty years I have continually seen; people who are making precisely that same mistake. I often wish I could see the younger people, and would that the Academy had been filled tonight with our high school scholars and our grammar school scholars, that I could have them to talk to.

I would have preferred such an audience as that because they are most susceptible; having not grown up into their prejudices as we have; having not gotten into any custom that they cannot break; and having not met with any failures as we have. I would have preferred such an audience because I could, perhaps, do such an audience as that more good than I can do grown-up people, yet I will do the best I can with the material I have.

I say to you that you have "acres of diamonds" in Philadelphia, right where you now live. The opportunity to get rich, to attain great wealth, is here in Philadelphia now, within the reach of almost every man and woman who hears me speak tonight, and I mean just what I say.

I have not come to this platform, even under these circumstances, to recite something to you. I have come to tell you what, in God's sight, I believe to be the truth. And if the years of life have been of any value to me in the attainment of common sense, I know that what I am to say is right. That is that the men and women sitting here, who found it difficult perhaps to buy a ticket to this lecture or gathering tonight, have within their reach "acres of diamonds," the opportunity to get largely wealthy.

There never was a place on earth more adapted than the city of Philadelphia today, and never in the history of the world did a poor man or woman, without capital, have such an opportunity to get rich quickly and honestly as he or she has now in our city. I say it is the truth, and I want you to accept it as such. For if you think I have come to simply recite something, then I would better not be here. I have no time to waste in any such talk, but to say the things I believe, and unless some of you get richer for what I am saying tonight, my time is wasted. I say that you ought to get rich, and it is your duty to get rich.

How many of my pious brethren say to me, "Do you, a Christian minister, spend your time going up and down the country advising young people to get rich, to get money?" "Yes, of course I do." They say, "Isn't that awful! Why don't you preach the gospel, instead of preaching about making money?" I answer that by saying that to make money honestly is to preach the gospel. That is the reason. The people who get rich may be the most honest men and women you find in the community.

"Oh," but says some young man here tonight, "I have been told all my life that if a person has money, he is very dishonest and dishonorable and mean and contemptible." My friend, that is the reason why you have none, because you have that idea of people. The foundation of your faith is altogether false. Let me say here clearly, and say it briefly, though subject to discussion which I have not time for here, ninety-eight out of one hundred of the rich people of America are honest. That is why they are rich. That is why they are trusted with money. That is why they carry on great enterprises and find plenty of people to work with them. It is because they are honest men and women.

Says another young man, "I hear sometimes of people who get millions of dollars dishonestly." Yes, of course you do, and so do I. But they are so rare a thing that the newspapers talk about them all the time as a matter of news, until you get the idea that all the other rich people got rich dishonestly. My friend, you take and drive me—if you furnish the auto—out into the suburbs of Philadelphia. Introduce me to the people who own their homes around this great city, those beautiful homes with gardens and flowers, those magnificent homes so lovely in their art. And I will introduce you to the very best people in character, as well as in enterprise, in our city; and you know I will.

People are not truly successful, until they own their own home. And those that own their homes are made more honorable, honest, pure, true, economical and careful, by owning that home. For a person to have money, even in large sums, is not an inconsistent thing. We preach against covetousness—and you know we do—

in the pulpit. We oftentimes preach against it so long and use the terms about "filthy dollars" so extremely, that Christians get the idea that when we stand in the pulpit, we believe it is wicked for *any* person to have money. That is, however, until the collection basket goes around, and then we almost swear at the people, because they don't give more money.

Oh, the inconsistency of such doctrines as that! Money is power, and you ought to be reasonably ambitious to have it. You ought because you can do more good with it than you could without it. Money printed your Bible, money builds your churches, money sends your missionaries, and money pays your preachers, and you would not have many of them either, if you did not pay them. I am always willing that my church should raise my salary, because the church that pays the largest salary always raises it the easiest. You never knew an exception to it in your life. The person who gets the largest salary can do the most good with the power that is furnished to them. Of course, if their spirit be right, they should use it for whatever reason they choose.

I say, then, you ought to have money. If you can honestly attain riches in Philadelphia, it is your Godly duty to do so. It is an awful mistake of these pious people to think you must be awfully poor, in order to be pious.

Some people say, "Don't you sympathize with the poor people?" Of course I do, or else I would not have been lecturing these years. What I sympathize with is that the number of poor who are to be sympathized is very small. To sympathize with people whom God has punished for their sins, and to help them when God continues a just punishment is to do wrong. No doubt about it! And we do that more than we help those who are deserving.

While we should sympathize with God's poor—that is, those who cannot help themselves—let us remember there is not a poor person in the United States who was not made poor by his or her own shortcomings, or by the shortcomings of some one else. It is all wrong to be poor anyhow. Let us give in to that argument and pass that to one side.

A gentleman gets up back there and says, "Don't you think there are some things in this world that are better than money?" Of course I do, but I am talking about money now. Of course, there are some things higher than money. Oh yes, I know by the grave that has left me standing alone that there are some things in this world that are higher and sweeter and purer than money. Well, do I know there are some things higher and grander than gold?

Love is the grandest thing on God's earth, but fortunate the lover who has plenty of money. Money is power, money is force, money will do good as well as harm. In the hands of good men and women, it could accomplish—and it has accomplished—good. I hate to leave that behind me.

I heard a man get up in a prayer meeting in our city and thank the Lord he was "one of God's poor." Well, I wonder what his wife thinks about that? She earns all the money that comes into that house, and he smokes a part of that on the veranda. I don't want to see any more of the Lord's poor of that kind, and I don't believe the Lord does. And yet, there are some people who think in order to be pious, you must be awfully poor and awfully dirty. That does not follow at all. While we sympathize with the poor, let us not teach a doctrine like that. Yet the age is prejudiced against advising for the attainment of wealth.

The prejudice is so universal and the years are far enough back, I think, for me to safely mention that years ago up at Temple University there was a young man in our theological school who thought he was the only pious student in that department. He came into my office one evening and sat down by my desk, and said to me: "Mr. President, I think it is my duty, sir, to come in and labor with you."

Said he, "I heard you say that you thought it was an honorable ambition for a young man to desire to have wealth, and that you thought it made him temperate, made him anxious to have a good name, and made him industrious. You spoke about man's ambition to have money helping to make him a good man. Sir, I have come to tell you the Holy Bible says that 'money is the root of all evil.' "

I told him I had never seen it in the Bible, and advised him to go out into the chapel and get the Bible, and show me the place. So out he went for the Bible, and soon he stalked into my office with the Bible open, with all the bigoted pride of the narrow sectarian or one whose spiritual foundation is based on some misinterpretation of Scripture. He flung the Bible down on my desk and fairly squealed into my ear, "There it is, Mr. President; you can read it for yourself."

I said to him: "Well, young man, you will learn when you get a little older that you cannot trust another denomination to read the Bible for you. You belong to another denomination. You are taught in the theological school, however, that emphasis is clarification. Now, will you take that Bible and read it yourself, and give the proper emphasis to it?"

He took the Bible, and proudly read, "The love of money is the root of all evil." Then he had it right, and when one does quote aright from that same old Book, he quotes the absolute truth.

I have lived through fifty years of the mightiest battle that old Book has ever fought. I have lived to see its banners flying free. For never in the history of this world did the great minds of earth so universally agree that the Bible is true—all true—as they do at this very hour.

Therefore, I say that when he quoted right, of course he quoted the absolute truth. "The love of money is the root of all evil." The person who tries to attain unto it too quickly, or dishonestly, will fall into many snares, no doubt about that. The love of money. What is that? It is making an idol of money. And idolatry, pure and simple, is condemned everywhere by the Holy Scriptures and by man's common sense.

The person who worships the dollar instead of thinking of the purposes for which it ought to be used; the person who idolizes simply money; the miser who hordes their money in the cellar, hides it in their stocking, refuses to invest it where it will do the world good; that person who hugs the dollar until the eagle squeals has in them the root of all evil.

I think I will leave that behind me now and answer the question nearly all of you are asking, "Is there opportunity to get rich in Philadelphia?"

Well, now, how simple a thing it is to see where it is. And the instant you see where it is, it is yours.

Some old gentleman gets up back there and says, "Mr. Conwell, have you lived in Philadelphia for thirty-one years and don't know that the time has gone by when you can make anything in this city?"

"No, I don't think it is," I reply.

"Yes, it is," shouts the old gentleman, "I have tried it."

"What business are you in?" I ask.

"I kept a store here for twenty years, and never made

over a thousand dollars in the whole twenty years," states the gentleman.

"Well, then," I said, "you can measure the good you have been to this city, by what this city has paid you, because a person can judge very well what he or she is worth by what he or she receives. That is, in what that person is to the world at this time."

If you have not made over a thousand dollars in twenty years in Philadelphia, it would have been better for Philadelphia if they had kicked you out of the city nineteen years and nine months ago. A person has no right to keep a store in Philadelphia twenty years and not make at least five hundred thousand dollars, even though it is a corner grocery uptown.

You say, "You cannot make five hundred thousand dollars in a store now." Oh, my friends, if you will just take only four blocks around you, and find out what the people want and what you ought to supply them. Set it all down with your pencil and figure up the profits that you would make if you did supply them with what they wanted, and you would very soon see it. There is wealth right within the sound of your voice.

Someone says: "You don't know anything about business. A preacher never knows a thing about business." Well, then, I will have to prove that I am an expert. I don't like to do this, but I have to do it because my testimony will not be taken, if I am not an expert.

My father kept a country store, and if there is any place under the stars where a man or woman gets all sorts of experience—in every kind of mercantile transactions—it is in the country store. I am not proud of my experience, but sometimes when my father was away, he would leave me in charge of the store, though fortunately for him that was not very often. But this did occur many times, friends: A man would come in the store and say to me, "Do you keep jackknives?"

"No, we don't keep jackknives," I would reply, and then I would be off whistling a tune. What did I care about that man, anyhow?

Then another farmer would come in and say, "Do you keep jackknives?"

"No, we don't keep jackknives," I would answer. Then I went away and whistled another tune.

Then a third man came right in the same door and said, "Do you keep jackknives?"

"No. Why is everyone around here asking for jack-knives? Do you suppose we are keeping this store to supply the whole neighborhood with jackknives?"

Do you carry on your store like that in Philadelphia? The difficulty was I had not then learned that the foundation of godliness and the foundation principle of success in business are both the same precisely.

The person who says, "I cannot carry my religion into business" advertises him or herself as being either an imbecile in business, on the road to bankruptcy, or a thief; one of the three for sure. That person will fail within a very few years. They certainly will, if they don't carry religion into business. If I had been carrying on my father's store on a godly plan, I would have had a jackknife for the third man, when he called for it. Then I would have actually done him a kindness, and I would have received a reward myself, which it would have been my duty to take.

There are some over pious people who think that if you take any profit—on anything that you sell—that you are an unrighteous person. On the contrary, you would be a criminal to sell goods for less than they cost. You have no right to do that. You cannot trust a person with your money who cannot take care of his or her own. You cannot trust a person in your family who is not true to his or her own spouse. You cannot trust a person in the world who does not begin with his or her own heart, own character, and own life.

It would have been my duty to have furnished a jack-knife to the third man, or the second, and to have sold it to him and actually profited myself. I have no more right to sell goods without making a profit on them than I have to overcharge him dishonestly beyond what they are worth. But, I should sell each bill of goods and make as much as I can honestly make. To live and let live is the principle of the gospel and the principle of everyday common sense.

Oh, hear me; live as you go along. Do not wait until you have reached my years before you begin to enjoy anything of this life. If I had the millions back, or fifty cents of it, which I have tried to earn in these years, it would not do me anything like the good that it does me now, in this almost sacred presence tonight.

Oh, yes, I am paid over and over a hundredfold tonight for dividing as I have tried to do in some measure, as I went along through the years. I ought not to speak that way; it sounds egotistic, but I am old enough now to be excused for that. I should have helped my fellowman, which I have tried to do, and everyone should try to do and get the happiness of it. The person who goes home with the sense that he or she has stolen a dollar that day and robbed someone of what was their honest due is not going to sweet rest. This person will arise tired in the morning and go to work the next day with an unclean conscience. This is not a successful person at all, although he or she may have laid up millions. But the person who has gone through life dividing always with his fellow man; making and demanding his or her own rights and his or her own profits, and giving to every other man or woman their rights and profits, lives every day. And not only that, but that is the royal road to great wealth. The history of the thousands of millionaires shows that to be the case.

The man over there who said he could not make anything in a store in Philadelphia has been carrying on his store on the wrong principle. Suppose I go into your store tomorrow morning and ask, "Do you know neighbor A, who lives one square away at house No. 1240?"

"Oh yes, I have met him," says the man. "He deals here at the corner store."

I ask, "Where did he come from?"

The man replies, "I don't know."

I ask, "How many does he have in his family?"

"I don't know," comes the answer.

I ask, "What ticket does he vote?"

Again the reply is, "I don't know."

I ask, "What church does he go to?"

The man answers, "I don't know and don't care. What are you asking all these questions for?"

If you had a store in Philadelphia, would you answer me like that? If so, then you are conducting your business just as I carried on my father's business in Worthington, Massachusetts. You don't know where your neighbor came from when he moved to Philadelphia, and you don't care. If you had cared, you would be a rich person now. If you had cared enough about him to take an interest in his affairs, to find out what he needed, you would have been rich. But, you go through the world saying, "There is no opportunity to get rich" and there is the fault right at your own door.

But another young man gets up over there and says, "I cannot take up the mercantile business."

(While I am talking of trade, it applies to every occupation.) I ask, "Why can't you go into the mercantile business?" "Because I haven't any capital," comes the reply.

 Oh, the weak and dudish creature that can't see over their collar! It makes a person weak to see these little people standing around the corners and saying, "Oh, if I had plenty of capital, how rich I would get."

I ask, "Young man, do you think you are going to get rich on capital?"

He answers confidently, "Certainly!"

Well I say, "Certainly not!"

If your mother has plenty of money, and she will set you up in business, you will "set her up in business," supplying her with capital. The moment a young person gets more money than he or she has grown to by practical experience, that moment he or she has gotten a curse. It is no help to a young man or woman to inherit money. It is no help to your children to leave them money, but if you leave them education, if you leave them noble character, if you leave them a wide circle of friends, if you leave them an honorable name, it is far better than that they should have money.

It would be worse for them, worse for the nation, that they should have any money at all. If you have inherited money, don't regard it as a help. It will curse you through your years, and deprive you of the very best things of human life. There is no class of people to be pitied so much as the inexperienced sons and daughters of the rich of our generation. I pity the rich man's children. They can never know the best things in life. One of the best things in our lives is when young people has earned their own living, become engaged and then make up their minds to own a home. Then with that same love comes also that divine inspiration toward better things, and they begin to save money. They begin to leave off the bad habits and put money in the bank. When they have a few hundred dollars, they go out in the suburbs to look for a home. They go to the savings bank perhaps, for half of the value, and then when the young man takes his bride over the threshold of that door for the first time, he says in words of eloquence my voice can never touch: "We have earned this home ourselves. It is all ours." That is the grandest moment a human heart may ever know.

However, a rich man's child can never know that. A rich young man takes his bride into a finer mansion and then is obliged to say to his wife, "My mother gave me this, my mother gave me that, and my mother gave me this" until his wife wishes she had married his mother. I pity them.

The statistics of Massachusetts showed that not one rich man's son or daughter out of seventeen ever dies rich. I pity the rich man's children, unless they have the good sense of the elder Vanderbilt, which sometimes happens. He went to his father and said, "Did you earn all your money?" Vanderbilt replied, "I did, my son. I began to work on a ferry-boat for twenty-five cents a day." "Then," said his son, "I will have none of your money." He too, tried to get employment on a ferryboat that Saturday night. He could not get one there, but he did get a place for three dollars a week. Of course, if a rich man's child will do that, he or she will get the discipline of a poor child that is worth more than a university education to any man or woman. They would then be able to take care of their father's millions.

However, as a rule, the rich will not let their children do the very thing that made them great. As a rule, they will not allow their children to work. Why, they would think it was a social disgrace if their poor, weak, little lily-fingered, sissy sort of a boy or bratty, uptight, snobbish little girl had to earn their living with honest toil. I have no pity for such rich men's children.

I remember once at Niagara Falls, but first, I think I remember one a great deal nearer. I think there are gentlemen present who were at a great banquet, and I beg pardon of his friends. At a banquet here in Philadelphia, there sat beside me a kind-hearted young man, and he said, "Mr. Conwell, you have been sick for two or three years. When you go out, take my limousine, and it will take you up to your house on Broad Street." I thanked him very much, and perhaps I ought not to mention the incident in this way, but I follow the facts. I got on to the seat with the driver of that limousine outside, and when we were going up I asked the driver, "How much did this limousine cost?"

"Six thousand, eight hundred dollars, and he had to pay the tax on top of that," said the driver.

"Well," I said, "does the owner of this machine ever drive it himself?" At that, the chauffeur laughed, so heartily that he lost control of his machine. He was so surprised at the question that he ran up on the sidewalk and around a corner lamppost out into the street again. And, when he got out into the street, he laughed until the whole machine trembled. He then exclaimed, "Does he drive this machine? Oh, he would be lucky if he knew enough to get out when we got to where we were going."

Back to Niagara Falls, I must tell you about a rich man's son. I came in from my lecture to the hotel, and as I approached the desk of the clerk, there stood a millionaire's son from New York. He was an indescribable specimen of anthropologic potency. He had a skullcap on one side of his head, with a gold tassel in the top of it, and a gold-headed cane under his arm with more in it than in his head. It is a very difficult thing to describe, that young man. He wore an eyeglass that he could not see through, patent leather boots that he could not walk in, and pants that he could not sit down in. He was dressed like a grasshopper. This human cricket came up to the clerk's desk just as I entered, adjusted his unseeing eyeglass, and spoke in this way to the clerk. You see, he thought it was High English, you know. He said, "Sir, will you have the kindness to supply me with some papah and envelophs!"

The hotel clerk measured that man quickly, and then he pulled the envelopes and paper out of a drawer, threw them across the counter toward the young man, and then turned away to his books. You should have seen that young man, when those envelopes came across that counter. He swelled up like a gobbler turkey, adjusted his unseeing eyeglass, and yelled: "Come right back here. Now sir, kindly order a servant to take those papahs and envelophs to yondah desk."

Oh, the poor, miserable, contemptible American monkey! He could not carry paper and envelopes twenty feet. I suppose he could not get his arms down to do it. I have no pity for such travesties upon human nature. If you have not capital, I am glad of it. What you need is common sense, not copper cents. The best thing I can do is to illustrate by the actual facts well known to you all.

A. T. Stewart, a poor boy in New York, had $1.50 to begin life on. He lost 87 and a half cents of that on the very first venture. How fortunate that young man who loses the first time he gambles. That boy said, "I will never gamble again in business," and he never did. So, how did he come to lose 87 and a half cents?

You probably all know the story of how he lost it. Because he bought some needles, threads, and buttons to sell which people did not want, and had them left on his hands, a dead loss. Said the boy, "I will not lose any more money in that way." So, he decided to go around first to the doors of those in his town and ask the people what they *did* want. Then, when he had found out what they wanted, he invested his 62 and a half cents to supply a known demand.

Study it wherever you choose in business, in your profession, in your housekeeping, whatever your life, that one thing is the secret of success. *You must first know the demand. You must first know what people need, and then invest yourself where you are most needed.* A. T. Stewart went on that principle until he was worth what amounted afterward to forty millions of dollars, owning the very store in which Mr. Wanamaker carries on his great work in New York. His fortune was made by his losing something, which taught him the great lesson that he must only invest himself or his money in something that people need.

When will you salespeople learn it? When will you manufacturers learn that you must know the changing needs of humanity, if you would succeed in life? Apply yourselves, as manufacturers or merchants or workmen to supply that human need. It is a great principle as broad as humanity and as deep as the Scripture itself.

The best illustration I ever heard was of John Jacob Astor. You know that he made the money of the Astor family when he lived in New York. He came across the sea in debt for his fare. But that poor boy with nothing in his pocket made the fortune of the Astor family on one principle.

Some young person here tonight will say, "Well, they could make those fortunes over in New York, but they could not do it in Philadelphia!" My friends, did you ever read that wonderful book of Riis (his memory is sweet to us because of his recent death) wherein is given his statistical account of the records taken in 1889 of 107 millionaires of New York? If you read the account, you will see that out of the 107 millionaires only seven made their money in New York. At that time, out of the 107 millionaires worth ten million dollars in real estate, 67 of them made their money in towns of less than 3,500 inhabitants. The richest man in this country today, if you read the real estate values, has never moved away from a town of 3,500 inhabitants. It makes not so much difference *where* you are as *who* you are. But, if you cannot get rich in Philadelphia, you certainly cannot do it in New York.

Now John Jacob Astor illustrated what can be done anywhere. He had a mortgage once on a millinery store, and they could not sell bonnets enough to pay the interest on his money. So he foreclosed that mortgage, took possession of the store, and went into partnership with the very same people, in the same store, with the same capital. He did not give them a dollar of capital. They had to sell goods to get any money. Then he left them alone in the store, just as they had been before, and he went out and sat down on a bench in the park in the shade.

What was John Jacob Astor doing out there, and in partnership with people who had failed on his own hands? He had the most important and, to my mind, the most pleasant part of that partnership on his hands. For as John Jacob Astor sat on that bench, he was watching the ladies as they went by; and where is the man who would not get rich at that business?

As he sat on the bench, he would wait for a lady to pass by him. He would then study her bonnet, and by the time she and the bonnet were out of sight, Astor knew the shape of the frame, the color of the trimmings, and the crinklings in the feather. I sometimes try to describe a bonnet, but not always. I would not try to describe a modern bonnet. Where is the man who could describe one? This aggregation of all sorts of driftwood stuck on the back of the head, or the side of the neck, like a rooster with only one tail feather left. But in John Jacob Astor's day there was some art about the millinery business, and he went to the millinery store and said to them: "Now, put into the show window just such a bonnet as I describe to you, because I have already seen a lady who likes such a bonnet. Don't make up any more until I come back."

Then he went out and sat down again, and another lady passed him of a different form, of different complexion, with a different shape and color of bonnet. "Now," said he, "put such a bonnet as that in the show window." He did not fill his show window up with a lot of hats and bonnets to drive people away, and then sit on the back stairs and bawl because people went to Wanamaker to trade. He did not have a hat or a bonnet in that show window, but what some lady liked *before* it was made up. The tide of custom began immediately to turn in, and that has been the foundation of the greatest store in New York in that line, and still exists as one of three stores. Its fortune was made by John Jacob Astor after they had failed in business, not by giving them any more money, but by finding out what the ladies liked for bonnets before they wasted any material in making them up.

I tell you if a man could foresee the millinery business, he could foresee anything under heaven! Suppose I were to go through this audience tonight and ask you, in this great manufacturing city, if there are not opportunities to get rich in manufacturing. "Oh yes," some young man says, "there are opportunities here still, if you build with some trust and if you have two or three millions of dollars to begin with as capital." Young man, the history of the breaking up of the trusts by that attack upon "big business" is only illustrating what is now the opportunity of the smaller man. The time never came in the history of the world when you could get rich so quickly manufacturing without capital as you can now.

But you will say, "You cannot do anything of the kind. You cannot start without capital." Young man, let me illustrate for a moment. I must do it. It is my duty to every young person, because we are all going into business very soon on the same plan. *Remember, if you know what people need, you have gotten more knowledge of a fortune than any amount of capital can give you.*

There was a poor man out of work living in Hingham, Massachusetts. He lounged around the house until one day his wife told him to get out and work, and as he lived in Massachusetts, he obeyed his wife. He went out and sat down on the shore of the bay and whittled a soaked shingle into a wooden chain. His children that evening quarreled over it, and he whittled a second one to keep peace.

While he was whittling the second one, a neighbor came in and said: "Why don't you whittle toys and sell them? You could make money at that."

"Oh," he said, "I would not know what to make."

Said his neighbor, "Why don't you ask your own children right here in your own house what to make?"

"What is the use of trying that?" said the carpenter, "My children are different from other people's children."

(I used to see people like that when I taught school.)

However, he acted upon the hint, and the next morning when his daughter came down the stairway, he asked, "What do you want for a toy?" She began to tell him she would like a doll's bed, a doll's washstand, a doll's carriage, a little doll's umbrella, and went on with a list of things that would take him a lifetime to supply. So, consulting his own children, in his own house, he took the firewood, for he had no money to buy lumber, and whittled those strong, unpainted Hingham toys that were for so many years known all over the world. That man began to make those toys for his own children, and then made copies and sold them through the boot-and-shoe store next door. He began to make a little money, and then a little more, and Mr. Lawson is believed to be the richest man in old Massachusetts, and I think it is the truth.

That man is worth a hundred million dollars today. For thirty-four years, he has been doing so on one principle: that one must judge what his own children like at home and what other people's children would like in their homes. To judge the human heart by oneself, by one's wife or by one's children is the royal road to success in manufacturing.

"Oh," but you say, "didn't he have any capital?" Yes, a penknife, but I don't know that he had paid for that. When I spoke thus to an audience in New Britain, Connecticut, a lady four seats back went home and tried to take off her collar, and the collar-button stuck in the buttonhole. She threw it out and said, "I am going to get up something better than that to put on collars."

Her husband said, "After what Conwell said tonight, you see there is a need of an improved collar-fastener that is easier to handle. There is a human need; there is a great fortune. Now then, get up a collar-button and get rich." He made fun of her, and consequently made fun of me, and that is one of the saddest things which comes over me like a deep cloud of midnight sometimes—although I have worked so hard for more than half a century, yet how little I have ever really done.

Not withstanding the greatness and the handsome-ness of your compliment tonight, I do not believe there is one in ten of you that is going to make a million dollars because you are here tonight; but it is not my fault, it is yours. I say that sincerely. What is the use of my talking, if people never do what I advise them to do? When her hus-band ridiculed her, she made up her mind she would make a better collar-button, and when a woman makes up her mind she will, and does not say anything about it, she does it. It was that New England woman who invent-ed the snap button, which you can find anywhere now. It was first a collar-button with a spring cap attached to the outer side.

Any of you who wear modern waterproofs know the button that simply pushes together, and when you unbut-ton it, you simply pull it apart. That is the button to which I refer, and which she invented. She afterward invented several other buttons, and then invested in more, and then was taken into partnership with great factories. Now that woman goes over the sea every summer in her private steamship—yes, and takes her husband with her! If her husband were to die, she would have money enough left now to buy a foreign duke or count or some such title as that at the latest quotations.

Now, what is my lesson in that incident? It is this: I told her then, though I did not know her, what I now say to you, "Your wealth is too near to you. You are looking right over it." And she had to look over it, because it was right under her chin. I have read in the newspaper that a woman never invented anything. Well, that newspaper ought to begin again. Of course, I do not refer to gossip—I refer to machines—and if I did, I might better include the men. The newspaper could never appear, if women had not invented something. Friends, think. Ye women, think! You say you cannot make a fortune because you are in some laundry, or running a sewing machine, or walking before some loom, and yet you can be a millionaire, if you will but follow this almost infallible direction.

When you say a woman hasn't invented anything, I ask, who invented the Jacquard loom that wove every stitch you wear? Mrs. Jacquard. The printer's roller, the printing press, were invented by farmers' wives. Who invented the cotton gin of the South that enriched our country so amazingly? Mrs. General Greene invented the cotton gin and showed the idea to Mr. Whitney, and he, like a man, seized it.

Who was it that invented the sewing machine? If I would go to school tomorrow and ask your children they would say, "Elias Howe." He was in the Civil War with me, and often in my tent, and I often heard him say that he worked fourteen years to get up that sewing machine. However, his wife made up her mind one day that they would starve to death, if there weren't something or other invented pretty soon, and so in two hours she invented the sewing machine. Of course, he took out the patent in his name. Men always do that.

Who was it that invented the mower and the reaper? According to Mr. McCormick's confidential communication so recently published, it was a West Virginia woman, who did so after McCormick and his father had failed altogether in making a reaper and gave it up. This woman took a lot of shears and nailed them together on the edge of a board, with one shaft of each pair loose, and then wired them, so that when she pulled the wire one way it closed them, and when she pulled the wire the other way it opened them, and there she had the principle of the mowing machine. If you look at a mowing machine, you will see it is nothing but a lot of shears.

If a woman can invent a mowing machine; if a woman can invent a Jacquard loom; if a woman can invent a cotton-gin; if a woman can invent a trolley switch—as she did and made the trolleys possible; if a woman can invent, as Mr. Carnegie said, the great iron squeezers that laid the foundation of all the steel millions of the United States, we men can invent anything under the stars! (I say that for the encouragement of the men.)

Who are the great inventors of the world? Again, this lesson comes before us. The great inventor sits next to you, or you are the person yourself. "Oh," but you will say, "I have never invented anything in my life." Neither did the great inventors, until they discovered one great secret. The really great person is a plain, straightforward, everyday, common sense man or woman. You would not dream that he or she was a great inventor, if you did not see something he or she had actually done. Their neighbors do not regard them as so great. You never see anything great over your back fence. You say there is no greatness among your neighbors. It is all away off somewhere else. Their greatness is ever so simple, so plain, so earnest, so practical, that the neighbors and friends never recognize it.

True greatness is often unrecognized. That is sure. You do not know anything about the greatest men and women. I went out to write the life of General Garfield, and a neighbor, knowing I was in a hurry, and as there was a great crowd around the front door, took me around to General Garfield's back door and shouted, "Jim! Jim!" And very soon "Jim" came to the door and let me in, and I wrote the biography of one of the grandest men of the nation, and yet he was just the same old "Jim" to his neighbor. If you know a great man in Philadelphia and you should meet him tomorrow, you would say, "How are you, Sam?" or "Good morning, Jim." Of course you would. That is just what you would do.

One of my soldiers in the Civil War had been sentenced to death, and I went up to the White House in Washington—sent there for the first time in my life—to see the President. I went into the waiting room and sat down with a lot of others on the benches, and the secretary asked one after another to tell him what they wanted. After the secretary had been through the line, he went in, and then came back to the door and motioned for me. I went up to that anteroom, and the secretary said, "That is the President's door right over there. Just rap on it and go right in."

I never was so taken aback, friends, in all my life, never. The secretary himself made it worse for me, because he had told me how to go in and then went out another door to the left and shut that. There I was, in the hallway by myself before the President of the United States of America's door. I had been on fields of battle, where the shells did sometimes shriek and the bullets did sometimes hit me, but I always wanted to run. I have no sympathy with the old man who says, "I would just as soon march up to the cannon's mouth as eat my dinner." I have no faith in a man who doesn't know enough to be afraid, when he is being shot at. I never was so afraid when the shells came around us at Antietam as I was when I went into that room that day; but I finally mustered the courage. I don't know how I ever did, but at arm's length, I tapped on the door. The man inside did not help me at all, but yelled out, "Come in and sit down!"

Well, I went in and sat down on the edge of a chair, and I wished I were in Europe. The man at the table did not look up. He was one of the world's greatest men and was made great by one single rule. Oh, that all the young people of Philadelphia were before me now and I could say just this one thing, and that they would remember it. I would give a lifetime for the effect it would have on our city and on civilization.

Abraham Lincoln's principle for greatness can be adopted by nearly all. This was his rule: Whatsoever he had to do at all, he put his whole mind into it and held it all there, until that was all done. That makes men and women great almost anywhere. He stuck to those papers at that table and did not look up at me, and I sat there trembling. Finally, when he had put the string around his papers, he pushed them over to one side and looked over to me, and a smile came over his worn face.

He said, "I am a very busy man and have only a few minutes to spare. Now tell me in the fewest words what it is you want." I began to tell him, and mentioned the case, and he said: "I have heard all about it and you do not need to say any more. Mr. Stanton was talking to me only a few days ago about that. You can go to the hotel and rest assured that the President never did sign an order to shoot a boy under twenty years of age, and never will. You can say that to his mother anyhow."

Then he said to me, "How is it going in the field?"

I said, "We sometimes get discouraged."

And he said: "It is all right. We are going to win out

now. We are getting very near the light. No man ought to wish to be President of the United States, and I will be glad when I get through. Then Tad and I are going out to Springfield, Illinois. I have bought a farm out there and I don't care if I again earn only twenty-five cents a day. Tad has a mule team, and we are going to plant onions." Then he asked me, "Were you brought up on a farm?"

I said, "Yes, in the Berkshire Hills of Massachusetts." He then threw his leg over the corner of the big chair and said, "I have heard many a time, ever since I was young, that up there in those hills you have to sharpen the noses of the sheep in order to get down to the grass between the rocks." He was so familiar, so everyday, so farmer-like, that I felt right at home with him at once. He then took hold of another roll of paper, and looked up at me and said, "Good morning." I took the hint then, got up, and went out.

After I had gotten out, I could not realize I had seen the President of the United States at all. However, a few days later, when still in the city, I saw the crowd pass through the East Room, by the coffin of Abraham Lincoln. And when I looked at the upturned face of the murdered President, I felt then, that the man I had seen such a short time before, who was so simple a man, so plain a man, was also one of the greatest men that God ever raised up to lead a nation on to ultimate liberty. Yet, he was only "Old Abe" to his neighbors. When they had the second funeral, I was invited among others, and went out to see that same coffin put back in the tomb at Springfield. Around the tomb stood Lincoln's old neighbors, to whom he was just "Old Abe."

Of course, that is all they would say. Did you ever see a man who struts around altogether too large to notice an ordinary working mechanic? Do you think he is great? He is nothing but a puffed-up balloon, held down by his big feet. There is no greatness there. Who are the great men and women?

My attention was called the other day to the history of a very little thing that made the fortune of a very poor man. It was an awful thing, and yet because of that experience he—not a great inventor or genius—invented the pin that now is called the safety-pin, and out of that safety-pin made the fortune of one of the great aristocratic families of this nation. A poor man in Massachusetts who had worked in the nail-works was injured at thirty-eight, and he could earn but little money. He was employed in the office to rub out the marks on the bills made by pencil memorandums, and he used a rubber until his hand grew tired. He then tied a piece of rubber on the end of a stick and worked it like a plane. His little girl came and said, "Why, you have a patent, haven't you?" The father said afterward, "My daughter told me when I took that stick and put the rubber on the end that there was a patent, and that was the first thought of that." He went to Boston and applied for his patent, and every one of you that has a rubber-tipped pencil in your pocket is now paying tribute to the millionaire. No capital, not a penny did he invest in it. All was income, all the way up into the millions.

But, let me hasten to one other greater thought. "Show me the great people who live in Philadelphia." A gentleman over there will get up and say: "We don't have any great people in Philadelphia. They don't live here. They live away off in Rome or St. Petersburg or London or Manayunk or anywhere else, but here in our town."

I have come now to the heart of the whole matter and to the center of my struggle: Why isn't Philadelphia a greater city in its greater wealth? Why does New York excel

Philadelphia? People say, "Because of her harbor." I ask, why do many other cities of the United States get ahead of Philadelphia now?

There is only one answer, and that is because our own people talk down their own city. If there ever was a community on earth that has to be forced ahead, it is the city of Philadelphia. If we are to have a boulevard, talk it down; if we are going to have better schools, talk them down; if you wish to have wise legislation, talk it down; talk all the proposed improvements down. That is the only great wrong that I can lay at the feet of the magnificent Philadelphia that has been so universally kind to me. I say it is time that we turn around in our city and begin to "talk up" the things that are in our city, and begin to set them before the world as the people of Chicago, New York, St. Louis, and San Francisco do.

Oh, if we only could get that spirit out among our people, that we can do things in Philadelphia and do them well! Arise, ye millions of Philadelphians, trust in God and man, and believe in the great opportunities that are right here—not over in New York or Boston, but here—for business, for everything that is worth living for on earth. There was never an opportunity greater. Let us "talk up" our own city.

Great people get into office sometimes, but what this country needs is people who will do what we tell them to do. This nation—where the people rule—is governed by the people, for the people, and so long as it is, then the office holder is but the servant of the people, and the Bible says the servant cannot be greater than the master. The Bible says, "He that is sent cannot be greater than Him who sent Him." The people rule, or should rule, and if they do, we do not need the greater people in office. If the great men and woman in America took our offices, we would change to an empire in the next ten years. I know of a great many young women, now that woman's suffrage is coming, who say, "I am going to be President of the United States someday." I believe in women's suffrage, and there is no doubt but what it is coming, and I am getting out of the way. I may want an office by myself; but if the ambition for an office influences the women in their desire to vote, I want to say right here what I say to the young men, that if you only get the privilege of casting one vote, you don't get anything that is worthwhile. Unless you can control more than one vote, you will be unknown and your influence so dissipated as practically not to be felt.

This country is not run by votes. Do you think it is? It is governed by influence. It is governed by the ambitions and the enterprises which control votes. The young woman who thinks she is going to vote for the sake of holding an office is making an awful blunder.

That other young man gets up and says, "There are going to be great people in this country and in Philadelphia."

"Is that so? When?" I ask.

"When there comes a great war; when we get into difficulty through watchful waiting in Mexico; when we get into war with England over some frivolous deed, or with Japan or China or New Jersey or some distant country. Then I will march up to the cannon's mouth; I will sweep up among the glistening bayonets; I will leap into the arena and tear down the flag and bear it away in triumph. I will come home with stars on my shoulder, and hold every office in the gift of the nation, and I will be great," says this man.

To which I answer, "No, you won't!"

You think you are going to be made great by an office,

but remember that if you are not great before you get the office, you won't be great when you secure it. It will only be a burlesque, in that shape. We had a Peace Jubilee here, after the Spanish War. Out West they don't believe this, because they said, "Philadelphia would not have heard of any Spanish War, until fifty years hence." Some of you saw the procession go up Broad Street. I was away, but the family wrote to me that the tally-ho coach with Lieutenant Hobson upon it stopped right at the front door and the people shouted, "Hurrah for Hobson!" and if I had been there, I would have yelled too, because he deserves much more of his country than he has ever received. Suppose I go into school and ask, "Who sunk the Merrimac at Santiago?" If the boys answer me "Hobson," they will tell me seven-eighths of a lie. There were seven other heroes on that steamer, and they, by virtue of their position, were continually exposed to the Spanish fire, while Hobson, as an officer, might reasonably be behind the smokestack. You have gathered in this house your most intelligent people, and yet, perhaps, not one here can name the other seven men.

We ought not to teach history so. We ought to teach that however humble a person's station may be, if he or she does full duty in that place, that person is just as much entitled to the American people's honor as is the king upon his throne. But, we do not so teach.

I remember another illustration. I would leave it out but for the fact that when you go to the library to read this lecture, you will find this has been printed in it for twenty-five years. I shut my eyes—shut them closed—and lo! I see the faces of my youth. Yes, they sometimes say to me, "Your hair is not white; you are working night and day without seeming ever to stop; you can't be old." But when

I shut my eyes, like any other man of my years, oh, then come trooping back the faces of the loved and lost of long ago, and I know, whatever men may say, it is evening time.

I shut my eyes now and look back to my native town in Massachusetts, and I see the cattle show ground on the mountaintop; I can see the horse sheds there. I can see the Congregational church; see the town hall and moun-taineers' cottages; see a great assembly of people turning out, dressed resplendently, and I can see flags flying and handkerchiefs waving and hear bands playing. I can see that company of soldiers who had re-enlisted, marching up on that cattle show ground. I was but a boy, but I was captain of that company and puffed out with pride. A cambric needle would have burst me all to pieces.

Then I thought it was the greatest event that ever came to man on earth. If you have ever thought you would like to be a king or queen, you go and be received by the mayor. The bands played, and all the people turned out to receive us. I marched up that Common so proud at the head of my troops, and we turned down into the town hall. Then they seated my soldiers down the center aisle, and I sat down on the front seat. A great assembly of people—a hundred or two—came in to fill the town hall, so that they stood up all around. Then the town officers came in and formed a half-circle.

The mayor of the town sat in the middle of the plat-form. He was a man who had never held office before; but he was a good man, and his friends have told me that I might use this without giving them offense. He was a good man, but he thought an office made a man great. He came up and took his seat, adjusted his powerful specta-cles, and looked around, when he suddenly spied me sit-ting there on the front seat. He came right forward on the platform and invited me up to sit with the town officers. No town officer ever took any notice of me before I went to war, except to advise the teacher to thrash me, and now I was invited up on the stand with the town officers. Oh my! The town mayor was then the emperor, the king of our day and our time.

As I came up on the platform, they gave me a chair about this far, I would say, from the front. When I had got seated, the chairman of the Selectmen arose and came forward to the table, and we all supposed he would introduce the Congregational minister, who was the only orator in town, and that he would give the oration to the returning soldiers. But friends, you should have seen the surprise which ran over the audience, when they discovered that the old fellow was going to deliver that speech himself. He had never made a speech in his life, but he fell into the same error that hundreds of other men have fallen into. It seems so strange that people won't learn that they must speak their piece as children, if they intend to be orators when they are grown, but some seem to think all one has to do is to hold an office to be a great orator. So, the mayor came up to the front, and brought with him a speech, which he had learned by heart walking up and down the pasture . . . where he had frightened the cattle.

He brought the manuscript with him and spread it out on the table, so as to be sure he might see it. He adjusted his spectacles, leaned over it for a moment, marched back on that platform, and then came forward like this—tramp, tramp, tramp. He must have studied the subject a great deal, when you come to think of it, because he assumed an "elocutionary attitude." He rested heavily upon his left heel, threw back his shoulders, slightly advanced the right foot, opened the organs of speech, and advanced his right foot at an angle of forty-five. As he stood in that elocutionary attitude, friends, this is just the way that speech went.

Some people say to me, "Don't you exaggerate?" That would be impossible. But I am here for the lesson and not for the story, and this is the way it went: "Fellow citizens . . . " As soon as he heard his voice, his fingers began to go like that, his knees began to shake, and then he trembled all over. He choked and swallowed and came around to the table to look at the manuscript. Then he gathered himself up with clenched fists and came back: "Fellow citizens, we are Fellow citizens, we are—we are—we are—we are—we are—we are very happy—we are very happy—we are very happy. We are very happy to welcome back to their native town these soldiers who have fought and bled—and come back again to their native town. We are especially—we are especially—we are especially. We are especially pleased to see with us today this young hero (that meant me), this young hero who in imagination (friends, remember he said that; if he had not said 'in imagination' I would not be egotistic enough to refer to it at all) this young hero who in imagination we have seen leading—we have seen lead-ing—leading. We have seen leading his troops on to the deadly breach. We have seen his shining—we have seen his shining—his shining—his shining sword—flashing. Flashing in the sunlight, as he shouted to his troops, 'Come on!'"

Oh dear, dear, dear! How little that good man knew about war. If he had known anything about war at all, he ought to have known what any of my G. A. R. comrades here tonight will tell you is true: It is next to a crime for an officer of infantry, in time of danger, to go ahead of his men.

"I, with my shining sword flashing in the sunlight, shouting to my troops, 'Come on!' "

I never did it. Do you suppose I would get in front of my men to be shot in front by the enemy and in the back by my own men? That is no place for an officer. The place for the officer in actual battle is behind the line. How often, as a staff officer, I rode down the line, when our men were suddenly called to the line of battle, and the Rebel yells were coming out of the woods, and shouted: "Officers to the rear! Officers to the rear!" Then, every officer gets behind the line of private soldiers, and the higher the officer's rank, the farther behind he goes. Not because he is any the less brave, but because the laws of war require that. And yet, he shouted, "I, with my shining sword."

In that house there sat the company of my soldiers who had carried that boy across the Carolina rivers that he might not wet his feet. Some of them had gone far out to get a pig or a chicken. Some of them had gone to death under the shell-swept pines in the mountains of Tennessee, yet in the good man's speech, they were scarcely known. He did refer to them, but only incidentally. The hero of the hour was this boy. Did the nation owe him anything? No, nothing then and nothing now. Why was he the hero? Simply because that man fell into that same human error, that this boy was great, because he was an officer and these were only private soldiers.

Oh, I learned the lesson then that I will never forget, so long as the tongue of the bell of time continues to swing for me. Greatness consists, not in the holding of some future office, but really consists in doing great deeds with little means and the accomplishment of vast purposes from the private ranks of life. To be great at all, one must be great here, now, in Philadelphia.

The person who can give to this city better streets and better sidewalks, better schools and more colleges, more happiness and more civilization, more of God, that person will be great anywhere. Let every person here, if you never hear me again, remember this, that if you wish to be great at all, you must begin where you are and what you are, in Philadelphia, now. The person who can give to this city any blessing; who can be a good citizen while he or she lives here; who can make better homes; be a blessing whether working in the shop, sitting behind the counter or keeping house; whatever be this person's life; this person—who would be great anywhere—must first be great . . . in their own Philadelphia.

MAKE THE MAGIC HAPPEN™

Your audience will walk away with information that they can immediately put to use.

M ake the Magic Happen is a customized 60–90 minute informative, inspirational, exciting, and fun presentation that has helped executives, employees, and sales reps of corporations, as well as leaders and members of associations, achieve their professional and personal goals.

Make the Magic Happen is filled with ideas and information that will help your audience to better understand and handle many of the "mental obstacles" that they face every day.

Some of the ideas and strategies that Bob offers are ways to:
- Unleash your mental power and overcome fear and negativity
- Welcome and embrace change
- Improve communication and teamwork and attitudes
- Understand the importance patience, dedication, and commitment

In a program designed *specifically for sales reps,* Bob also offers information on how to:
- Think like an entrepreneur
- Increase sales through the L.A.S.T principle and the 3 F's
- Look at what you sell from a new point of view and heighten presentational skills
- Become a self-motivator . . . and much more.

Bob works closely with your meeting and event staff to make sure that he understands your specific needs, concerns, and objectives. Then he clearly communicates those issues and provides usable ideas and strategies that he has personally used for over 20 years as a successful businessperson and entrepreneur.

Additionally, recognized as a world class magician, mindreader, and comedian, Bob uses these skills and talents in place of overheads and slides to creatively enhance specific information in each of his customized presentations. This unique style of delivery, as well as Bob's charisma and contagious enthusiasm, not only captures the minds and hearts of his audience, but also allows him to reinforce his message in a highly memorable way.

"Bob Garner is a speaker whose business knowledge, amazing talents, and superb presentational skills lift meetings, conferences, and events to new and dazzling heights."

For information on Bob Garner's
Make the Magic Happen™ presentation:

Call: 888.811.8465
U.S. Main: 805.534.1576
International: 01.805.534.1576

Or visit: www.bobgarner.com

SUNDAY & WEISS PUBLISHING QUICK ORDER FORM

4 ways to order:

1. Fax this form to: 805.534.1577
2. Call toll free: 888.811.8465 • Int'l: 01.805.534.1576 (**Please have credit card ready**)
3. Email: orders@sundayandweiss.com.
4. Mail this form to: Sunday & Weiss Publishing, P.O. Box 6001, Los Osos, CA, 93412

Large quantity orders receive a special discount. Contact Sunday & Weiss Publishing for more information.

Please send me: _____ copy (copies) of Masters of Motivation™ . . . $12.95 each*

***Sales tax:** Please add 7.25% for products shipped to California addresses.

***Shipping and handling:** Orders shipped usually within 3–5 business days by Priority Mail in US*.

United States: add $4.50 for first book and $2.50 for each additional product.

International: add $9.00 for first book and $4.00 for each additional product (estimate).

Total Amount: _____(U.S. funds only)

Name: _____ Phone: _____

Address: _____

City: _____ State: _____ Zip: _____ Country: _____

Payment: ❏ Check   ❏ Visa   ❏ MasterCard

Credit Card Account #: _____ Exp. Date: _____

Cardholder's Signature: _____

❏ Please keep me posted about other products from Bob Garner and Sunday & Weiss Publishing. Email address: _____

Orders made by personal check, please allow 3 weeks for delivery.
All credit card orders are secure. We will not sell, lease, or provide information to anyone with regard to your purchases.

www.sundayandweiss.com

Thank you for your order.